BLACKWATER DRAW

**Three Lives, Billy the Kid
and the
Murders that Started
the
Lincoln County War**

BLACKWATER DRAW

Three Lives, Billy the Kid
and the
Murders that Started
the
Lincoln County War

DAVID S. TURK

SUNSTONE
PRESS

SANTA FE

Sunstone books may be purchased for educational, business, or sales promotional use.
For information please write: Special Markets Department, Sunstone Press,
P.O. Box 2321, Santa Fe, New Mexico 87504-2321.

Book and Cover design • Vicki Ahl
Body typeface • Humanst521 BT
Printed on acid free paper

Library of Congress Cataloging-in-Publication Data

Turk, David S.
  Blackwater draw : three lives, Billy the Kid, and the murders that started the Lincoln
County War / by David S. Turk.
      p. cm.
  Includes bibliographical references.
  ISBN 978-0-86534-780-9 (softcover : alk. paper)
  1. Lincoln County (N.M.)--History--19th century. 2. Murder--New Mexico--Lincoln
County. 3. Billy, the Kid. 4. Frontier and pioneer life--New Mexico--Lincoln County.
I. Title.
  F802.L7T87 2011
  978.9'64--dc22
                          2010050696

Published in

WWW.SUNSTONEPRESS.COM
SUNSTONE PRESS / POST OFFICE BOX 2321 / SANTA FE, NM 87504-2321 /USA
(505) 988-4418 / ORDERS ONLY (800) 243-5644 / FAX (505) 988-1025

The Kid's Lawless [B]and
[By Lily Casey Klasner]

[I]

McS[w]ain the lawer [sic], Dick Brewer the Captian [sic], at their command,
Thirteen was the number of this cruel lawless band,
Who started out for vengence [sic], no justice at their hands,
They run on to Morton and Baker on the Pecos sands.

2

The two made a galant [sic] fight for lefe [sic], it was their last stand,
Being over powered and promised passports the safest in the land,
Then marched up the lonely Pecos, skiping [sic] the the [sic] main highway,
To the [C]hisum ranch at South Springs, there ended up their day,

3

They left the Chism [sic] Ranch just at the break of day,
Haulting [sic] at Roswell which happened to be on the way,
Then headed for the [C]apitan the roughest mountain way,
Reaching Blackwater Draw and there without delay.

4

They fouly [sic] murdered McCloskey for being in their way,
Also killed Morton and Baker while on their knees to pray,
Then rode to the town of Lincoln that very same day,
To see Lawer [sic] Mc[Sween] who was waiting to give them their pay.

5

They left these human bodies for the wild kyotes [sic] to prey,
A way out in the foot hills where they fell that day,
Very depraved, even worse than the savage in his day,
Would have been guilty of an act more dastardly in its way.

—From the Lily Casey Klasner Papers, L. Tom Perry Special Collections,
Harold Lee Library, Brigham Young University, Provo, Utah. Despite the
spelling errors and truncated verse, this was the poetic version of the events.

CONTENTS

INTRODUCTION——9

PROLOGUE
How the Blackwater Murders Started the Lincoln County War——13

1 — THE CANYON MEANS DEATH——21

2 — A VIRGINIA BOY GOES WEST——40

3 — TWO HIDDEN LIVES
Frank Baker, AKA Hart and William McCloskey——57

4 — THE TUNSTALL MURDER WHODUNIT——77

5 — THE CAPTURE AND TRAIL TO BLACKWATER——90

6 — DAMNATION OF THE REGULATORS——105

7 — A SHOVELFUL OF FATE——116

EPILOGUE
Looking for Them——124

REPORT OF ANALYSIS, AGUA NEGRA SPRINGS——130

BIBLIOGRAPHICAL SUMMARY ON SOURCES——134

NOTES——138

DEDICATION

This book is dedicated to two late friends: Lionel (Lonnie) Lippmann, photographer, artist, husband and humanitarian; and Walter Dollahon, screenwriter, filmmaker, radio personality and family man. They started on this adventure, and while they are no longer with us, this book invokes the spirit and influence they embodied.

INTRODUCTION

No conflict, internal or external in our nation's history, was as complex as the Lincoln County War. Atrocious acts were committed by monied interests of both sides, one firmly grounded in New Mexico Territory's political base and the other trying to profit as relative newcomers. At its base, the Lincoln County War was not about colorful personalities. It was about money and power. In this instance, the money was invested in beef contracts and the sides stocked with personalities that outsized the actual purpose of the clashes.

The names of Billy the Kid, Jessie Evans, John Henry Tunstall and William Brady dominated any conversation of the Lincoln County War. The Kid, then William Bonney in the early segment of the conflict, touched almost every aspect in the series of conflicts. Bonney was a vengeful cowhand who was ready for a fight. However, the snake-like canyons of Lincoln County harbored other colorful characters, who like Bonney, came from elsewhere to end up gripping a gun. The names of William S."Buck"Morton, Frank Baker, or William McCloskey are footnotes in most accounts of the Lincoln County War. They disappeared after the first chapters, as do many of the men who pursued, captured, and later killed them.

The murders of Morton, Baker, and McCloskey were critical to the chronology and heightened conflict of the Lincoln County War. The Kid remained a villain as chronicled during their murders in a canyon known as Blackwater. However, the murders themselves, which claimed victims from both sides, represented the powder keg that started the Lincoln County War rather than the singular murder of John Henry Tunstall. Although this statement on its face seems ridiculous, the Tunstall murder reached Washington and London, was heavily covered by the press, and was investigated by a federal agent from the Justice Department. The citizens of New Mexico Territory saw the three Blackwater deaths as an outpouring of angst. Before the murders, the cause of the conflict was firmly the prominence of business. Tunstall was a British citizen and adventurer who had been in the area scarcely more than a year. All three of the Blackwater victims resided in the area longer and were not rich landowners or cattle barons.

To understand the importance of this singular day, March 9, 1878, and separate it from the confusing and overbearing events that occurred, both victims and captors need to be studied. The questions that needed answers were: How did they get to Blackwater Canyon and the draw where the action took place? How was the reaction handled differently from the Tunstall murder? Most importantly, how did the chain of events that followed directly reflect the Blackwater Canyon murders rather than the Tunstall murder? The confusing nature of the three deaths led to several events thereafter, escalating the Kid on to further fame. The Tunstall murder proved Bonney little more than a close associate, which gave him a motive for shooting Buck Morton and Frank Baker, but those motives already existed through bad experiences in his past employment with them.

In this volume, I combined personal research conducted on numerous personalities and their participation in the Lincoln County War. As the collection of material and new findings grew, they took on a larger life of their own. Long-standing historical questions were answered, and the research in this volume shed new light on an overlooked corner of the Lincoln County War. The lives and deaths of the three men followed a twisting path also trodden by Billy the Kid and his Regulators at the beginning of the series of gun battles.

To be certain, this work does not address all questions, such as what happened in Fort Sumner in July 1881, when tradition stated Lincoln County Sheriff Patrick Garrett shot Billy the Kid. That is left for others to answer. Instead, the lives, capture, and death of William S. "Buck" Morton and his two fellow victims are studied. The related movement of their captors, in context to the killings in Blackwater Canyon on March 9, 1878, was found in the details.

My search for the three victims—Morton, Frank Baker, and William McCloskey in Blackwater Canyon—began with a letter. When reading Morton's neat penmanship on his farewell letter to a cousin, Judge Hunter Holmes Marshall, the writing revealed his educated hand. The content was a plea, stating that if something should befall him, his brother Quin, residing in Lewisburg, West Virginia, should be notified. That town was a place my own grandfather frequented as a youth.

Quin Morton actually resided several miles from Lewisburg in the community of Ronceverte, an old logging town along the Greenbrier River. Members of the Morton family and my ancestors were buried in the same cemetery. We were connected by these neighborly bonds. His conversion from scion of a blue blood family to a wandering cattleman yielded more material relating to his past.

Morton's twisted path ran from his past. In the course of my research, the backgrounds of the other victims, Frank Baker and William McCloskey, became partially apparent. Both had pasts more mysterious than Morton. As most historians concluded, Baker was an alias. As a hidden figure, it was difficult to piece together his past. At least several misconceptions that were previously published were clarified. McCloskey was a man with fewer clues than Baker, but only vague ones. In fact, except in the case of his death, the old man was barely noticed in historical texts.

Having experience with this kind of historical study, I saw some unique opportunities in researching this portion of the Lincoln County War. Part of my intent was to add something new, either fresh research or logical sequence. Once shared by a fellow historian, I faithfully assigned myself to the statement: "The object of history is to bring the ghosts into the room and make them speak."

Undoubtedly some of this material has been featured in other publications, but its presentation draws new conclusions. As years passed, more media became available, better methodologies developed and more papers and pictures emerged from private hands. I visited those private hands, and did not restrict myself to archival or published material. In order to complete the study, source material was found far beyond New Mexico. In fact, much was found in Alabama, Arkansas, Kansas, Missouri, Oklahoma, Texas, and Virginia. I sought the obscure pieces, much like Colonel Maurice Fulton, Robert N. Mullin and Philip Rasch did in their work on the Lincoln County War.

Morton, Baker, and McCloskey—or their captors—were not just figures on a movie screen. They had flesh and blood beliefs and problems. The captors were not just evil characters, and their own stories were rarely pretty. Their motives were hardly similar—some were victims of circumstance while others sought revenge. Few of them had the same reason for being in Blackwater Canyon on March 9, 1878. The violent nature of the frontier they worked, coupled with the basic philosophy of an "eye for an eye," ensured almost none lived to a ripe, old age. To get a complete picture, a path was carved out to get to Blackwater Canyon.

In my opinion, the murders of these three men, rather than the equally tragic death of British subject and businessman John Henry Tunstall, set the key explosion that ignited the Lincoln County War. The book concludes with my two searches for the bodies of the three murdered cowboys in Blackwater Draw. In July and October 2006, I led two teams of subject experts and scientists into the field with the express goal of locating the bodies. There was evidence the bodies had been moved, as was discussed in several histories of the Lincoln County War. The results of the searches revealed an important correction in American history— exactly what happened at Blackwater Draw and how the three were murdered. Artifacts from the two searches were professionally analyzed, and the report revealed as an appendix to the text.

PROLOGUE

How the Blackwater Murders Started the Lincoln County War

When was the Lincoln County War? The dates of the string of conflicts varied, but most historians agreed that it occurred between early 1878 through the summer of 1879. A few writers stretched the timeline out further to the December 1880 capture of Billy the Kid at a stone house in Stinking Springs, a settlement near Fort Sumner. However, this was part of a separate campaign that began long after the bulk of the hostilities in Lincoln County, a large chunk of the southeast portion of the New Mexico Territory which then measured approximately 170 miles in each direction of the compass.[1]

Prior to the actual war was the conflict between the "landed gentry" of Lincoln and their financial backers in Santa Fe versus a group of independent ranchers and entrepreneurs. The powerful gentry controlled much of the commerce going in and around Lincoln County. The governor of the Territory, 59-year-old Samuel Beach Axtell, was part and parcel of the so-called "Santa Fe Ring," a shadowy group of officials and businessmen investing and profiting from their counterparts. Axtell was in his third year at the post, and the Ring had been formed before this time. The two other primary members of the political arm of the enterprise were politicians Thomas Benton Catron and Stephen Benton Elkins. Both arrived in the New Mexico Territory in the mid-1860s and established a political machine that included lawyers, judges, lawmen, and merchants. This reached far beyond Santa Fe and affected the large cattle trade in Lincoln. There, mercantile interests of the Ring included former soldiers Lawrence G. Murphy and Emil Fritz. They formed L.G. Murphy &

Company, which in time took on a sinister side name, "The House." In the early 1870s, they held the economic keys to the county. This underwent serious transition after Fritz died in June 1874. Murphy, a drinker of great proportions, continued on until March 1877, when his health broke. Taking their places were two of their young clerks, James J. Dolan and John H. Riley. They reformed the "House" as Jas. J. Dolan & Company. The 29-year-old Irish-born Dolan was a former New York Zouave, the Civil War unit that sported fiery red caps and pants into battle. The same daring that drove Jimmy Dolan into the Zouaves followed him to Lincoln. Riley, also a former soldier, contrasted Dolan by his work behind the scenes. Furthermore, he diversified his financial interests into other areas of the Territory. The "House" proved solid yet vulnerable in the wake of Murphy's retirement. It provided the path for partnering enterprises seeking their own paths of commerce.[2]

A newer and independent group of ranchers and settlers encompassed both large concerns such as Texas cattleman John Chisum and smaller semi-independent cattlemen like John Henry Tunstall and Richard Brewer. Tennessee native John Simpson Chisum was already a known cattleman in Texas who stretched his herds of longhorns into the plains of Lincoln County in the mid-1870s. One of the larger cattle barons of the Texas plains, he sought new grazing lands far from his rivals such as Charles Goodnight. Establishing South Spring Ranch in 1875, Chisum later sold most of his New Mexico herd to a St. Louis firm, but remained in charge. His brother James ran most of the daily operations on the ranch, located near a budding village. Later, this was known as the city of Roswell. James'daughter Sallie, then in her teens, stood out as a softer side to the hard-bitten cowboys of the Pecos Valley. Her youthful beauty, encapsulated in a tintype of the era, showed a confident girl with deep set eyes and sharp features. Sallie captured a romantic spirit in hard times. With her came permanancy and commitment to their new home. Overall, the move to New Mexico Territory was a success. Chisum's new prosperity meant another outside economic tie, this one in another state, and another rival for the Santa Fe Ring. Worse yet, he became potential competition for the lucrative beef contracts to the Mescalero Apache. It turned out Chisum was not the only rival.[3]

The Ring focused on the new cattle concerns of John Chisum, but the "House" had other potential rivals in Lincoln County. Most notable was John Henry Tunstall, an enterprising young Briton in his twenties who appeared in Lincoln by late 1876.[4] New England native Brewer, aged twenty-five, came by way of Wisconsin and initially worked for the "House." His picture shows a youth with wavy brown hair yet beardless, a man trying to make it in the rough and tumble of Territorial New Mexico. By 1877, he broke with Jimmy Dolan over a sale to Tunstall. However, both the Chisum concern and the new independents like Tunstall and Brewer had a local ally of their own in Lincoln lawyer Alexander McSween.[5]

Canadian-born Alexander McSween had come to Lincoln County due to his health and became a formidable lawyer shortly after his March 1875 arrival in town. He zealously represented the "House," but broke with them over his success with Chisum. Like Brewer, Murphy and Dolan felt his actions amounted to betrayal. McSween would not do business on their terms. In fact, his religious and ethical bars were considered high for the Territory. His wife Susan was a Pennsylvanian, small and slight with dark eyes and hair, an image contrasting her spouse's regal profile. Although their land was purchased from the "House," Dolan and Riley found themselves at odds with the couple over business.[6]

As events unfolded, it was business that created the rift which led to John Tunstall's death. With the "House" unable to dislodge Chisum or his independent allies, who actually battled among themselves during the short-lived Pecos War in 1876–77, their tactics became more forceful over time. The transition of leadership from Murphy and Fritz to Dolan and Riley also impacted the business relationships. While shrewd, Dolan's inclination to "balance the books" on his own terms was integral to the heightened violence. Both sides had cowhands, such as William Bonney, known to history as Billy the Kid, who worked for them. Many had worked for both the "House" and either Chisum or the independents. Their loyalties were more personal and diverse, but they did not control events until after the Tunstall murder. Therefore, the Lincoln County War was in two parts, and the actual war began after the murders in Blackwater Canyon. There it became personal and controlled by the cowboys rather than the cattle owners. Still, the chronology seemed uninterrupted and neatly packaged that historians and enthusiasts alike found it easier to lump them together into one long conflict.

With this logic in mind and the information known, the Lincoln County War can be broken down as follows:

- The murders of Buck Morton, Frank Baker, and William McCloskey in Blackwater Canyon on March 9, 1878.
- The heightened violence that followed, particularly ambushes, the fight at Blazer's Mill, and the murder of Lincoln County Sheriff William Brady in April 1878.
- Judge Frank W. Angel's inquiry into the death of Tunstall. While the death was business gone amuck, the cowboys gave the depositions in the summer of 1878.
- The so-called "Five-Day Battle" in Lincoln, instigated by heightened anger towards McSween and the cowhands. This culminated in the death of McSween and others in July 1878.
- Intervention by the Territorial Governor and the declining period of violence from March 1879.

The Lincoln County War began as a reaction to the murders of Morton, Baker, and McCloskey. The survivors involved in one portion of the conflict were largely the same as the other. Billy the Kid was present in almost every instance. Both the death of Tunstall and the Blackwater murders involved cowhands from the same two sides of the conflict, those of the "House" and the outsiders, and both ended in violence and death. Tunstall's plight was a tragedy, but it was a political murder based on economic threat. Worse yet, it likely happened by mistake. The addition of several violent fugitives to the party pursuing Tunstall muddled the message the "House" wanted to send. It would have been far easier to follow the pattern of discouragement they were giving Tunstall and fellow cattleman John Chisum than killing a noted British subject whose death aroused international implications. Indeed, there was a greater incentive to push Tunstall out and secure the Mescalero beef contracts for the "House." In contrast, the deaths of the three men in Blackwater Canyon proved opposite. It was personal and not linked to business at all. Morton had fired and may have cheated the Kid in the past, while Baker conspired in the same effort. McCloskey, who abhorred violence, was an inconvenient roadblock to a grudge.

The violent episodes that followed Blackwater remained personal. The ambush and deaths of several of the capturing party, notibly Frank MacNab, and of Lincoln County Sheriff William Brady, were personal matters. Tempers rose to a fever pitch when the noted Regulators, the followers of the independent concerns, felt their justification for killing the three was rendered moot by a rigged legal process controlled by the Santa Fe Ring. When the British pressed the Justice and State Departments to look into Tunstall's death, it forced the hand of Washington to get involved. Special Agent Frank Warner Angel traveled to the New Mexico Territory and deposed the participants in the Tunstall murder. These depositions touched on the singular instance of the Tunstall murder and rarely strayed into any other reactive episode. He took these depositions in the early summer of 1878, just before the so-called "Five-Day Battle," when Sheriff George W. Peppin of Lincoln County and military authorities from nearby Fort Stanton pressed a comprehensive campaign against the Regulators. The death of several citizens, including Alexander McSween, branded the county. Amid the backdrop of the heightening violence, Angel conducted his work methodically. To him, as with many, the deaths in Blackwater Canyon were a consequence, a postscript to the Tunstall murder. Angel was in Lincoln for approximately three weeks, hardly time to ascertain the motives of the angry cattleman and vengeful merchants, let alone analyze the crime.

When a new territorial governor, Lew Wallace, took over after

Axtell was removed from the position, he wanted an end to the violence. Meeting Billy the Kid face to face in March 1879, Wallace offered Bonney a pardon, but this never occurred. With this, the Lincoln County War officially ended. By doing this, Governor Wallace, then obsessed with writing a novel, *Ben Hur*, solved both side-by-side conflicts. The personal and business aspects were wiped clean, as the latter proved embarrassing to any effectual law. By then, the "Five-Day Battle" and the ambush death of Brady in town dominated the lion's share of press attention rather than the deaths of Morton, Baker, and McCloskey. The fight was out of them and Lincoln County was considered damaged goods. McSween, Tunstall, and Brewer were dead and John Chisum consumed with problems. The newcomers were mortally wounded, but the operational structure of the "House" and the Santa Fe Ring notably damaged. Axtell was gone and there was a chance to start fresh. Fritz and Murphy both passed away, leaving Jimmy Dolan as the "House" leader.

The Lincoln County War ended, and the personalities who started the conflict spread throughout the region. The Kid and several other Regulators ended up in Tascosa, Texas, a cowtown in the Panhandle. He eventually returned to Lincoln and took part in a rustling and counterfeiting operation with Billy Wilson, a mysterious character who emerged from Texas. His December 1880 capture at Stinking Springs ended his relationship with the enterprise. Several of his fellow Regulators were not so lucky, as they met their death in a shootout. The Kid was imprisoned and brought back to Lincoln to hang. However, he escaped and killed the officers that transported him. Finally, history dwelled on his showdown with Lincoln County Sheriff Pat Garrett at Fort Sumner on July 14, 1881. The most famous Regulator faded into history. However, several former Regulators from Blackwater Canyon died in their beds at an old age.

With such a large cast of characters and events, the division between motives at Blackwater Canyon were lost in a maze of linked events. Separating the Tunstall murder from the Blackwater murders required a close study of both events. However, history emphasized the former of these two situations while largely casting the other aside as a consequence. Blackwater Canyon was where things became personal, and then controlled, by the cowhands, so this is where the Lincoln County War actually started.

1

THE CANYON MEANS DEATH

In the late afternoon of March 9, 1878, a caravan of riders stopped at a spring called Aqua Negra, or "Black Water." The rough-looking group stopped to water their horses and quench their thirst. The narrow trail they followed was primarily used by local sheep herders and cowhands. It stretched northwest from the dusty little village of Picacho to the town of Lincoln, a distance of approximately twenty miles. The road was long and circuitous, a route that ran along the Capitan Mountains, bone dry and chock full of sturdy brush and rattlesnakes. Low spiked cactus lined the sides of the thin dirt strip. In earlier times, the Mescalero Apache tribe occupied this valley. It was one of their roving hunting encampments. Blackwater served as an oasis in an otherwise arid frontier. The large spring, known as the "Black Water Holes" or "Blackwater Draw," provided water for ranch settlers and animals alike. The canyon and its contiguous territory made good grazing lands, and an alternative route to the busier main road between the towns of Lincoln and Roswell.

For the group of thirteen men riding on that hot afternoon, the journey was horrible. Two men were captives. One was a young boss of a cow camp in the Pecos River Valley, William S. "Buck" Morton, and the other a notorious cowhand named Frank Baker. There were eleven captors by name. The leader of the group was a rancher named Richard Brewer. The others, who had scattered origins, were Josiah G. "Doc" Scurlock, Charlie Bowdre, William "Kid" Bonney, Henry Newton Brown, Frank MacNab, Fred Waite, Sam Smith, Jim French, William McCloskey, and John Middleton. They started about ten o'clock that morning from cattleman John Simpson Chisum's South Spring Ranch near Roswell. By nightfall, they were expected in Lincoln. There, the eleven were to transfer their two prisoners to the custody of the county sheriff as suspects in the death of their late ally, British citizen and rancher John Henry Tunstall.[1]

The riders spread out along the road, and some a good distance from the others. The two prisoners rode on horses side by side. Brewer rode in the rear when he heard a sudden burst of gunfire. By the time he reached the front, both prisoners and William McCloskey lay dead on the canyon floor. Brewer was unhappy, as the burden fell on him to speak to the authorities and arrange burial. Once he approached a sheepherder's camp near the spring, he supposedly bargained with a few local men to do the job. One of the herders that day was a 22-year-old farm hand named Francisco Gutierrez. He and his fellow herders knew the area, primarily populated by Spanish-speaking families. Gutierrez and his companions dug several adequate graves.[2]

Much of the agreement ends on what happened after the killings. Depending on who is believed, much reconstruction was needed. Marshall Ashmun Upson, Roswell's postmaster and former reporter, popularly known as Ash, gave a highly-publicized account through his book with Patrick F. Garrett, *The Authentic Life of Billy the Kid*. However, it was Upson, as postmaster, who sent a last fateful letter for Buck Morton. It was he who gave detailed descriptions of the three men killed. Lastly, it was Upson who tied himself to several key figures in the Lincoln County War. To his credit, he was candid in his letters home. Historian Maurice Fulton, among others, researched this angle and provided some of the surviving information.

McCloskey and Middleton constantly rode close upon the prisoners as if to protect them; the others brought up the rear, except the Kid and Bowdre, who were considerably in advance. About twenty or thirty miles from Roswell, near the Black Water Holes, McNab and Brown rode up to McCloskey and Middleton. McNab placed his rifle to McCloskey's head, 'You are the s— of a b— that's got to die before harm can come to these fellows are you?' and fired as he spoke. McCloskey rolled from his horse a corpse.

The terrified, unarmed prisoners fled as fast as their sorry horses could carry them, pursued by the whole party and a shower of harmless lead. At the sound of the shot, the Kid wheeled his horse. All was confusion. He couldn't take in the situation. He heard fire-arms, and it flashed across his mind that perhaps the prisoners had in some unaccountable manner got possession of weapons. He saw his mortal enemies attempting to escape, and he sank his spurs into his horse's sides he shouted to them to hault [sic], but they held on their course with bullets whistling around them. A few bounds of the infuriated grey carried him to the front of his pursuers. Twice only his revolver spoke, and a life sped at each report. Thus died McCloskey, and thus perished Morton and Baker.[3]

The *Mesilla Independent* and *Santa Fe New Mexican* published a letter the same day, March 16, 1878. From the notes of Colonel Fulton, the letter was penned by Upson, as he was one of the last to see the three men alive.[4]

FROM LINCOLN COUNTY
Three Men Killed
Two of the Banditti Wiped Out!
Roswell, N.M. March 10 1878:

Editors Independent:

Richard Bruer [sic] and a constable's posse, with legal process, arrested WM. S. Morton and Frank Baker on the bank of the Pecos after a 5 mile chase. The prisoners are chanrged [sic] with the killing of J.H. Tunstall. The posse arrived at Chisum's ranche [sic] on Friday 8th inst. Left for Roswell where Morton registered a letter about 10 o'clock on Saturday morning. Morton, at the Postoffice

[sic] expressed fears that he would be lynched, and declared his willingness to stand trial. About half past ten o'clock the party left with their prisoners ostensibly for Lincoln. About five o'clock P.M. on the same day, Martin Chaves reported that the party had left the road on thieir [sic] left and gone towards Black Water Holes. This, Sunday evening, about dusk, Frank McNab, one of the arresting party, returned. His statement of events after leaving here are in substance as follows:—

"When we had ridden some 20 miles, and had reached a point some 5 or 6 miles from Black Water, Morton was riding side by side with one of the posse McCloskey, when he suddenly snatched McCloskey's pistol from the scabbard and shot him dead."

"Although mounted upon a poor slow horse, he put him to his best speed closely followed by Frank Baker, they were speedily overtaken and killed."

McNab said as he had no further business in that direction he returned. Whatever faze [sic] (phase) or color future developments may put upon the fact of the affair, there is no doubt but that McCloskey, Morton, and Baker are killed.[5]

In the 1930s, the Works Progress Administration (WPA) gathered historical accounts of the Lincoln County War. An interesting interview with San Patricio, New Mexico resident Francisco Trujillo related key elements of the murders. He was well-versed as to who Baker and Morton were, although as many in this area, he backed Billy the Kid's men in their actions. Baker was documented as a member of an outlaw gang before his untimely death. Trujillo's account of the deaths varied little from that of Fulton. He stated that "one of the gang named McLoska [sic] said that he preferred to be shot himself rather than to have one of those men killed. No sooner had he said this, when he found himself shot behind the ear. After they killed McLoska [sic], Frank Baker and Billy Mote [sic] were promptly executed."[6]

While the WPA and Fulton accounts are similar, there was a second construction of events, a "Regulator's account," largely fueled by affidavits from Government Agent Frank Angel's investigation of Tunstall's death later in 1878. The reliability of the accounts, which officially made Morton and Baker villains instead of victims, was only partially believable. The deponents wanted to cover their actions, and the diversity of accounts signaled that some told different stories. These particular statements were peppered with a shade that favored their own actions. Not one of the accounts said—"I did it because things got botched up." There was plenty of confusion. Secondly, the depositions were gathered by parties that favored one side or the other. An example was the deposition of John Middleton, who was present when Morton, Baker, and McCloskey were killed, and sworn to the Justice of the Peace, "Squire" John B. Wilson. This account reads specifically:

> I was one of the <u>posse</u> who arrested Frank Baker and W. Morton aforesaid at J.J. Dolan &Co's Cow Camp in the Pecos during the month of March, 1878.... When within 25 miles of the town of Lincoln, Morton drew a revolver out of McCloskey's side they riding side by side, said McCloskey being one of said <u>posse</u>, and shot said McCloskey in the head. Baker had a pistol concealed. Morton & Baker then made every effort to escape, and refusing to halt were fired upon and killed about half a mile from where McCloskey was killed. I have related all I know about said affairs.[7]

Several points made these official accounts suspect. There was little chance of Baker concealing a weapon during the journey. Morton may have made a run for it, but McCloskey was a moderate who favored imprisonment to death. This fact was known to Morton himself, and it made McCloskey's death suspicious. There was reason for Bonney or MacNab to fear McCloskey as a rogue element in their party.

George Washington Coe, who fought on the side of the Regulators, but was not present in their party during the capture, asked Billy the Kid about the deaths later. The answer was chilling. Coe rarely spoke of it, but did say, "Of course, you know, George, I never meant to let them birds reach Lincoln alive."[8]

This was verified by Trujillo's account. The Kid's personal alliances with numerous Spanish-speaking families in Picacho and San Patricio shaded the account in favor of his actions. The account stated that the decision to kill Morton and Baker came after the capture. Trujillo said, "Later when they talked it over further with the rest, it was again decided to kill them but not to bring them to Lincoln."[9]

If Trujillo's account is true, then Bonney committed premeditated murder. However, a question arose on when the decision to kill was actually made. The death of McCloskey, coupled with the actions of Middleton and Brewer, contended that there was a division in intent. Brewer was the man in charge of bringing the prisoners to Lincoln, and there appeared to be nothing that signaled otherwise in his actions. The background of Brewer was that of an honest businessman whose cattle partially vanished, stolen by Dolan allies. He was no cold-blooded killer. Middleton, who came from Kansas, personally knew McCloskey and probably hesitated to kill him. A severe wound received at a gunfight several weeks later at Blazer's Mill sped his hasty departure from Lincoln County within a few months.[10]

Florencio Chaves, a Regulator who assisted in the capture of the two men, stated that there was a plan to kill Morton and Baker, but that McCloskey would not go along with it. While riding along the Picacho Road, the three riding in front: Bonney, Waite, and Big Jim French, communicated with others by a simple switch in riding positions. Waite, according to Chaves, dropped back within earshot of Scurlock, who suggested a test for the old man. He then asked McCloskey, "What's the best way to kill those sons a bitches?" McCloskey insisted they proceed to the sheriff. French then blocked the old man from the front, and Henry Brown drew his gun and shot McCloskey point blank. Morton and Baker bolted, knowing they were next to die. The problem in Chaves' testimony lay in the lack of details mentioning the actions of Brewer, Middleton, and MacNab. All three were present, but the key assailant was MacNab. He was positioned alongside, but one thing was clear. Either Henry Brown or Frank MacNab killed McCloskey.[11]

The masquerade continued after the murders. The three lay motionless on the rocky canyon floor, left where they fell. Bonney and most of the Regulators headed for the safety of San Patricio or Roswell, but Brewer had warrants in his hand. He could not avoid the responsibility of reporting their deaths in Lincoln. Once there, Brewer related the attempted escape and the unfortunate results to a lawyer and authorities. Further, he hired several sheepherders to bury the men.[12]

MacNab made his way to Roswell, where he encountered Ash Upson in the Post Office on March 11th. Upson said "Hello McNab, I thought you were in Lincoln by this time. Any news?" He replied in the affirmative, and said, "Morton killed McCloskey, one of our men, and made a break to escape, so we had to kill them." Upson got inquisitive, which was not surprising given his journalistic background. "Where did Morton get weapons?" MacNab told Upson that "He [Morton] snatched McCloskey's pistol out of its scabbard and killed him with it, and ran, firing back as he went. We had to kill them or some of us would have been hurt."[13]

According to Maurice Fulton, Ash Upson doubted MacNab's story. This was revealed later, in his role as ghostwriter of several key chapters in 1882's *Authentic Life of Billy the Kid*. It was McCloskey and Middleton who rode closest to the prisoners. MacNab and Brown approached from the rear, while Bonney and Charlie Bowdre rode out in front. However, Upson was unsure of either Bonney's or Bowdre's role in the murders. The shells found in Blackwater Canyon lay bunched together, indicating the captors stood close to each other. A large number of guns fired from the same location at a common target. A few stray cartridges were found between the encampment and two tombstone-shaped rocks. The two broke and ran abruptly, passing Bonney and Bowdre, who were closest to them at that point.[14]

Either Baker or Morton fell after the first volley. The trace failed to relate who made it to the rocks. Most accounts noted Morton as the last victim. Miguel Otero, later Governor of New Mexico, wrote his own account in *The Real Billy the Kid* (1936). He claimed it was the Kid's own account.[15]

It had been resolved, by two or three of the posse, to murder Morton and Baker before they reached Lincoln. McCloskey and Middleton constantly rode close behind the prisoners, as if to protect them; the others brought up the rear. Charlie Bowdre and I were at all times in advance. About twenty-five or thirty miles from Roswell, near Aqua Negra Spring, Frank McNab and Hendry Brown rode up to McCloskey and Middleton. McNab placed his revolver to McCloskey's head and said: 'You're the bastard that's got to die before harm can come to these fellows, are you?' and fired as he spoke. McCloskey rolled from his horse, a corpse. The prisoners fled as fast as their ponies could carry them, pursued by the whole party and a shower of harmless lead. At the sound of the first shot, I wheeled my horse and saw everything in confusion. I heard firearms, and it flashed across my mind that perhaps the prisoners, in some unaccountable manner had gotten possession of some weapons. I saw the two prisoners attempting to escape, so I put my spurs to my horse's sides and shouted to them to halt, but they held on their course, with bullets whistling around their heads. A few bounds of the gray carried me to the front of the two prisoners, who were doing their best to get away. I fired once at Morton and once at Baker, and they both fell dead from their horses.

The Kid dismounted, turned Morton's face up to the sky, and gazed down on his old companion. He asked no questions and the party rode on to Lincoln, except McNab, who returned to Chisum's ranch. The bodies remained where they had fallen, and were afterward buried by some Mexican sheep herders.[16]

One lone cartridge shell lay near the rocks. Although it was likely not from the shootout, as this shell variety was used a year later, Morton probably died there, at the only natural protection available to him, aside from the cactus and land crevices. History favored the Kid as the shooter of the final bullet. This was bolstered by the fact he was one of the closest to the fleeing men. Charles Russell's famous drawing of the murders, which depicted the victims on foot and close together, in a vain attempt to avoid the Kid's final bullets, was another imaginative but accurate scenario. One of the two victims faced down while the other fell forward, as the Kid sat atop a horse, his rifle having done its work. Although the cactus resembled Arizona's tall version rather than the short, dense type that dotted Blackwater Canyon, the pursuers rode on horseback.[17]

The Kid gave his own account of the deaths in an official affidavit upon the return of the warrants. This slightly varied version of events from Otero's account was faithfully recorded in William E. Hamlin's 1959 contrarian account of the Lincoln County War, *The True Story of Billy the Kid*. Within it, the outlaw commented on his own "official" account of the Blackwater Canyon killings. The Kid apparently worked through lawyer McSween, and his version was later seconded by Brewer. It was very close to the Otero account and wording, and in fact it nearly duplicated the former's words.

We knew some members of the posse were determined to kill Morton and Baker on the way back to Lincoln. I hadn't wanted to take them prisoners, but, since they were, I didn't want to kill unarmed men, either. I had hoped they would take their chances and come out of that old house fighting like men. I knew Baker to be a coward, but Morton was a real fighting man, even if he did shoot Tunstall. Brewer had given his word, and, while I didn't like it and cussed him plenty, I intended to help him carry it out. When we left Roswell, we believed the three riders who had escaped us before would head for Dolan's ranch and return with a bunch of warriors to free Morton and Baker and give us some hell, so we were plenty careful.

McCloskey and Middleton rode close beside the prisoners. Brewer had told Middleton to watch McCloskey, for he didn't trust him. Charlie Bowdre and I scouted some distance ahead, while the rest of the posse acted as a rear guard. About thirty miles from Roswell, Frank McNab and Hendry Brown rode up to McCloskey and Middleton. Frank put his gun close to McCloskey's head, saying, "So you're the damned bastard who said you'd have to be killed before anything can happen to these _hombres_."

McNab fired as he spoke, and McCloskey fell from the saddle, dead. Middleton had no chance to interfere, and, if he had, he'd have been killed, too. I heard the one shot and turned to see what had happened, and saw Morton and Baker in a full gallop, away from the group. There was confusion. A number of the possemen were milling around the spot where McCloskey had fallen, while others, led by Dick Brewer, were riding after the prisoners, firing as they rode.

My first thought was that Morton and Baker had somehow got guns—maybe from McCloskey—and made their break. I expected them to separate, which would have been good sense, so I told Bowdre to follow Baker and I would look after Morton, but they stuck together.

I was riding Old Grey, and he is some ground-gainer. I cut across at an angle and yelled to them to pull up. Morton only waved his hand, and they both spurred their horses, hard. I was still out of range, but I forced Old Grey to shorten the distance while I got my rifle from the boot. When I got within less than a hundred yards of them, I pulled up short and dismounted to aim. I fired twice, first at Baker, then at Morton. I got them both – pretty lucky shots. Perhaps it was just as well, for I'm certain, had they reached Lincoln, Brady would have arranged their escape. That is just the way it all happened, Mr. McSween.[18]

A group shot of the Regulators. Nine were present at Blackwater Canyon during the murders. Lincoln Heritage Trust, Lincoln, New Mexico.

An analysis of the Kid's account of the murders brought out interesting differences among the other Regulator's testimony of the same event. There was no defense of MacNab in this account, and no attempt to blame Morton. In fact, the account was complimentary of him. Lastly, the Kid admitted his own involvement in the shooting without including a motive. There was no reason to admit wanting them dead, and the Kid used a self-defense posture. Despite the flimsy alibi, the account was partially true, as the large number of shells found in July 2006 proved. The Kid fired two shots. Otero's account confirmed that Bonney fired once at each prisoner. If measured, the actual evidence corroborated the Kid's account on this point. In conclusion, the Kid minimized his own involvement and motive. However, he gave a fairly accurate account given the evidence. Of the numerous accounts of the murders, this one was often dismissed or lost as contrived.[19]

Of all the affidavits of the three deaths, John Middleton gave the most unbelievable one. He contrasted his testimony from the Kid's words. Not surprisingly, other accounts similarly stretched the imagination. A news piece that appeared in the *Albuquerque Review* on March 30, 1878 gave a curious account, dated on March 14 by one "XYZ." In this column, another motive was given for the three murders. The intent was based on a point made in a proclamation by New Mexico Territorial Governor Samuel Axtell on March 9th. From this document, it appeared that the Santa Fe Ring, a fixed group of politicians and businessmen in control of the Territory, circled their wagons. Justice of the Peace John B. "Green" Wilson was stripped of his ability to try Morton and Baker for the Tunstall murder. The column stated that "two men went express from Green Wilson and stated that he could not try them as his commission had been taken away. Brewer and party then took the "Boys" about 60 miles to the foot of the "Captain" (mountains) and there murdered them."[20]

"XYZ," described as a "reputable citizen of Lincoln," tied the explanation of the Morton and Baker murders to Governor Axtell's Proclamation, and gave sympathy as the motive for the actions of the Regulators. Even McCloskey's death was related. The old herdsman objected to shooting the two men while they were tied, and threatened to testify against them, "XYZ" stated. Oddly, the writer claimed "Young Kid" Antrim shot him. Finally, "XYZ" stated in the last line that there "were 9 balls in Morton's body and I in his head; and five in Baker."[21]

"XYZ" wrote an important column, as it highlighted several disparities in accounts. If Morton had 9 balls and I in his head, he ran further than Baker and was the last one shot as reconstructed by the Kid's account. The five balls in Baker indicated that he fell first. Morton lasted at least one more volley than Baker. It was plausible that two of the Regulators checked with Wilson in Lincoln before taking the two prisoners there, and it explained the delay in deciding their fate. Once the Regulators knew they no longer had legal power to punish, they chose the only route open to them. However, "XYZ" was wrong about one fact. The Kid did not shoot McCloskey. Given the knowledge "XYZ" confessed, plus his insight on the lack of legal standing, pointed out that the writer was a lawyer, probably either Wilson or McSween.

The popular lore of the three deaths persisted over time. Exaggerated versions of the shooting emerged, some peppered with elements of storytelling in them. One such account, with the basic outline of the facts, was published in *Frontier Times* in January 1936. Max Coleman of Lubbock, Texas, was the author. It contained dialogue—with the oft-repeated phrase by the Kid: "Never fool with a fool." The article was primarily about Texan Andrew L. "Buckshot" Roberts, someone Coleman knew well. By contrast, his account of the three deaths was full of inaccuracies. First of all, the three died before "Buckshot" Roberts. Coleman mistakenly placed Roberts' death *before* their own, and it was nearly a month between the two incidents.

> "Shoot 'em down," yelled Billy the Kid. "I've stole cattle with them and know what they are. Besides, that's what they did to Tunstall."
>
> ...Baker and Morton were started for Lincoln, the Kid riding on the right, a young Texan on the left. Young Bonney, Baker, and

Morton railed at each other, they attempting to belittle his exploits. They came to a gate. The Kid dismounted, leaving his winchester [sic] in the saddle scabbard.

"Only a fool gets away from his gun," said Baker.

"Never fool with a fool," answered Bonney.

He went to open the gate. With the speed of a snake striking, Baker reached over, jerked the sixshooter from the scabbard of the other guard and shot him through the heart. As the report died the two were already turning their horses and as they spurred them with all their might, Baker said:

"Nothing to stop us but Billy, and he is just a kid."

But they had misjudged the buck-toothed youth, for screaming and cursing, his teeth snapping like a wolf, he wrenched the winchester [sic] from its scabbard and ten seconds later had started his career of killing under the name of Billy the Kid. For Baker and Morton lay dying, having been drilled through the back by his unerring marksmanship. It is said he rode up to them and Morton had not expired. The Kid remarked:

"That's how Tunstall felt. Enjoy yourself in hell! [sic]"[22]

The account made for great storytelling, but was inaccurate. The Texan alongside was supposed to be McCloskey. His death mirrored the "Regulator version" in a general fashion. The Kid carried a Winchester rifle, but the bullet cartridges found in Blackwater Canyon varied in type. A few were indeed period Winchester cartridges. The Kid was not directly beside the prisoners in any other account, but up in the lead. Logically, he had the best shot at them during an escape attempt. Finally, the dialogue was an enhanced device for the reader, especially the repeated phrase "never fool with a fool."

Coleman's article was a great example of "piggy-backing" in history. This process related various events as told in the past, or in some cases handed down as stories, and interwove them with oral history. Kernels of reality mixed with a storyteller's spice created an enticing myth. No doubt Coleman believed this account, and maybe even the dialogue. However, first-hand accounts were scarce. Some people believed more in the details written in the newspapers, despite the agendas. Worse yet, the encounter was passed on as told, sometimes to the well-meaning. The result was historical "piggy-backing," a practice that affected many accounts of the Kid and befuddled historians for decades. Ramon Adams, Maurice Fulton, Robert Mullin, Phil Rasch, Frederick Nolan, and later Don Cline and Joel Jacobsen, in _Such Men as Billy the Kid_, deciphered much of this from the actual happenings. It was not an easy task, as more oral history was collected through some vague or peppered accounts to the Works Progress Administration in the 1930s. In Billy the Kid's case, the mystique was _always_ there. Starting with the Garrett account, which many "piggy-backed" on, the details are still being scrutinized. Coleman's article had minimal historical value, and cannot be taken as serious scholarship. However, stripped to the basics, an investigative eye can decipher what really happened.

Burial

A short time after the murders, the sheepherders supposedly buried the three men. They were staunch Catholics, so certain religious observances were respected. Billy Patrick Charles wrote that March 6, 1878 was the beginning of Lent—Ash Wednesday. March 9th fell within this religious period, where fasting and attendance at ceremonies were required. The Spanish-speaking citizens of Picacho and San Patricio were particularly affected by these observances as centers of faith in the area. It was reasonably assumed that religious values played a role in the burial of the three men. The closest objects to tombstones were rocks, so it made sense that they buried them near the stones. One of the assistants in a Texas A&M research team examining the area in October 2006 revealed that the herders likely buried them on the eastern side of the rocks, as the sun rose in the east.[23]

There was a second theory about the burials. Instead of Brewer paying the sheepherders, the pursuing posse under Sheriff Brady and his deputy, Mathews, dug the graves themselves. Given more information, this seemed likely for the hasty initial burial. "XYZ," the anonymous writer, penned in the _Albuquerque Review_ that the "sheriff's party, Brady with them, came back today [March 14, 1878] after burying Billy Morton and Frank Baker."[24]

There was at least one account confirming the posse buried the three men. Milo Pierce, an ally of Morton and Baker, and a leader of a rescuing contingent, told Roswell resident James ("Uncle Jim") Miller that they located the horse tracks off the main road to Lincoln to trace the route. Pierce and a number of his men located the bodies.

After these fellows were killed, someone got lumber from a freighter and made three boxes and buried the three dead men apparently just where they fell. That was, as near as I remember, about three or four hundred yards apart, all by the road on the side of the road. The graves were so shallow that the dirt had blown off of one end and one corner of all the boxes could be seen. I passed by there ten years afterwards, hauling lumber to my farm, and could see the boxes, but some time later someone took them up.[25]

There were multiple accounts of reburial. John Meadows wrote in his manuscript _Early Experiences_ that he actually re-buried the bones, mauled by coyotes, not once but twice. The second time he stated that he buried them in "a pretty lttle [sic] valley ... HALF WAY BETWEEN THIRTEEN MILE LAKE AND BLACKWATER."[26] Fulton reported that Brewer sought local sheepherders and found one named Gutierrez. Even recently, a Lincoln County resident related that his great-uncle worked on the ranch and discovered a lone skeleton surface near the spring bank, which he covered. Regardless of which versions of burial and re-burial were more believable, they could have been placed together in one grave. The soil was rocky and hard, and the digging of two or three large holes of an adequate depth was difficult.[27]

Francisco Gutierrez, early Spanish sheepherder in the Hondo Valley. It was he who likely buried Buck Morton. Maurice G. Fulton Papers, Special Collections, University of Arizona.

Aside from their burial, word of the murders spread fast. In a Roswell market owned by Marion Turner and Heiskel Jones, two of Jones' sons discussed the killings. They related that McCloskey was a spy for Dolan's men and not a true Regulator. However, accounts about McCloskey's actions were enigmatic. He was overheard stating that he would not let harm come to the prisoners. As these were not guarded words, McCloskey was either a humanitarian or present to ensure the safe return of Morton and Baker. In neither of these cases was McCloskey called a spy, but that did not mean that Bonney felt otherwise.[28]

The echoes of the murders resounded in the continuation of the conflict between the two factions, which kindled the full-scale Lincoln County War. There was one real motive on the part of the Kid – revenge. Miller confirmed that motive in the *Roswell Record* in March 1928. He remembered the conversation in the Jones store in Roswell following the deaths of the three men. As he recently arrived from Colorado, "Uncle Jim" was a fresh face in the area and no one hesitated to talk with him. Storekeeper Jones, pointing to his ten-year-old boy, was "anxious to talk about his sons, John and Jim and the part they were likely to play in the 'war' because of their general reputation for 'saltiness'. That bit of paternal applause seemed to summarize the spirit of the times."[29]

Conclusion: Three Lives Crossed

It appeared that there was another motive for the deaths of Morton, Baker, and McCloskey: power. Largely generated by money, the retaliatory killings inspired a rivalry. The horrific murders motivated the participants on either side of the conflict and affected relationships in distant regions. When the three men lay dead, it ended one cycle of violence and began a new one. A simpler explanation that consistently arose was that the killings in Blackwater Canyon were "payback" for the death of Billy the Kid's ally, John Henry Tunstall. This explanation was not adequate. The facts pointed to the backgrounds of the three victims. Most knew each other before the capture, and each interrelated with the Kid and his Regulators. In each case, it was a toxic relationship.

When the major books on the Lincoln County War touched on the murders, the authors left little background of the victims. Two critical works that detailed the previous lives of the victims were found in Eve Ball's edition of the memoirs of Lincoln County resident Lily Casey Klasner, *My Girlhood Among Outlaws* (1972) and George W. Coe's *Frontier Fighter* (1934). The unintended device of historical "piggy-backing" or story-telling, occasionally interfered. *Frontier Fighter* was a great first-hand account, providing much material on the Lincoln County War. However, one relative, a great-granddaughter of Coe, acknowledged transcription differences arose during its dictation. A major mistake in the text, discussed later in the book, inherited from Walter Noble Burns' *Saga of Billy the Kid* (1926), was discovered. Despite this unintentional oversight, Coe's account was invaluable to all studies on the Lincoln County War. Overall, Ball's edition of the Klasner account was insightful to the actions of local inhabitants. In addition, it provided details on the lives of two of the three dead men. However, the origins of Klasner's work took a bizarre twist. While the facts are probably all in place, substantial authorship belonged to Sallie Chisum, the niece of cattle boss John Chisum, rather than Klasner herself. In her introduction to *My Girlhood Among Outlaws*, Ball believed Sallie Chisum Robert lost interest in the project of compiling a manuscript of the events. Discussions with Sallie's descendants did not bear this out at all. In fact, much of the material was "borrowed" by Klasner and never returned. She combined her memoirs with that of Sallie Chisum Robert to make one manuscript.[30]

As in all books, the devil was in the details. Both works greatly assisted in providing clues to the background of the three victims. Nonetheless, tracing those clues back proved difficult, and in some cases impossible. The backgrounds of the three victims could not have been more dissimilar. In the three victims, you have distinctly different examples of lifestyle. Buck Morton ran from misfortune in post-bellum Virginia. His life rapidly changed as he left a prominent family to become a ranch foreman. In Frank Baker, there was a man who allegedly took on a new identity and engaged in a series of robberies and adventures, often with colorful characters such as outlaw Jessie Evans. The last victim, William McCloskey, was an itinerant cowboy. He was not running from his past, but he paid for his peaceful aims. Three different men, but one fate ended them all.

2

A VIRGINIA BOY GOES WEST

The motive behind the murders lay hidden in circumstances that took place far before the tragedy. To understand how things got so personal, the lives of the victims must be recounted. The interaction of the captors and their victims crossed repeatedly, and the reactions resulted from their life experiences. The victims partially foreshadowed their own fates by their personalities.

Of the three men who lay dead in the canyon, Buck Morton left the most documentation. From his arrival in the West as a refugee from Virginia to his closing days as a tough boss of a cow camp, Morton suffered from his own bad choices. However, he showed the most promise of the three victims. Buck wandered for nearly a decade. Had the Civil War not intervened in the lives of the Morton family, he would have stayed east. The luckless Virginian fell into an environment rife with violence. However, it was in one of his final acts, the penning of a letter to a cousin, which sparked the growing reputation of Billy the Kid.

William S. Morton, the eldest child of eight, was born in 1855 in Marysville, later known as Charlotte Court House, Virginia. The tiny hamlet was the seat of Charlotte County, a half day's ride from the city of Petersburg. His father, David Holmes Morton, was a dry goods merchant who kept the village store. He was related to two of Virginia's most famous families, the Randolphs and Marshalls, and named for his cousin, David Holmes, the first governor of the State of Mississippi. Buck's mother, Joanna Cabell, was similarly connected, a relation to the notable Breckinridge and Bouldin families of Virginia. Buck's grandfather and great-grandfather were both physicians in the city of Lynchburg. The origin of his nickname was unknown, but dated early, as his father called him "Buck" in a January 1868 letter.[1]

The Morton family was instrumental in the community growth of Charlotte Court House. The founding of the town dated to the mid-Eighteenth Century, when a tavern and courthouse served as its social centers. The Morton family and their relatives purchased a large number of town tracts when the land sold in 1817. John Morton & Company, an enterprise owned by Buck's paternal grandfather, purchased lot number two, just opposite the public square. Two additional tracts were purchased by the family in partnership with others. Their Marshall relatives purchased three of the new tracts. Both families boasted prominent lawyers, businessmen, and gentlemen farmers. Although the town changed names twice more over the course of the next century, first to Smithville, the town finally settled on its original name of Charlotte Court House in 1901.[2]

In antebellum Charlotte County, life was generally peaceful and promising for the Morton family. The county's fertile fields allowed good crops. Plantations dotted the landscape with names like "Do Well" and the Marshall family seat, "Roxabel." In April 1860, David Morton broadened his business with licenses to sell beer, wine and spirits, without any objection from the courts due to his good character. He employed several clerks to work in his store, located near the public square.[3]

The Morton family and their relatives resided throughout the county—and Buck was named in court records long after he went west. One of those relatives was the famous orator John Randolph of Roanoke, who dominated politics in the region for decades. After the great orator's death in 1833, his estate was in litigation for decades. Randolph's estate papers extended to 1878, as they named Buck Morton in a county court summons dated only weeks prior to his murder.[4]

Buck Morton's family life during his early years was typical of the historical circumstances of his region. He received his early education from his maternal great-uncle, scholarly jurist Thomas Tyler Bouldin. In his famous last letter dated March 8, 1878, Buck Morton's stylish penmanship revealed his upbringing. Morton's maternal grandfather, Breckinridge Cabell, moved to the western Virginia settlement of Lewisburg in the early 1850s. An old frontier military post during the Revolutionary War, the Mortons and their relations adopted the area as their second home. Within two decades, it was their permanent home. They established connections to prominent families in Lewisburg, notably Buck's Aunt Sallie, who married into one of the area's founding families, the Stuarts. However, the practical reason for the move to Lewisburg was Breckinridge Cabell's occupation as a physician, and its close proximity to the area's recuperative springs. It was a sensible place for a doctor to open a practice, as many people sought recovery in its waters.[5]

The Civil War and its aftermath ruined the fortunes of the Morton family. David Holmes Morton joined the Confederate forces in a local unit, the Charlotte Cavalry. The unit was active throughout the war and saw battle in the Gettysburg and Appomattox campaigns. One of his Marshall cousins, Hunter Holmes Marshall, Jr., was killed in the latter campaign. However, the horrors of war paled when compared to the consequences afterward. Breckinridge Cabell, said to be despondent by the war, left for South America. David Morton's business closed, and he worried over money. He longed to send Buck for a formal education, but lacked the necessary funds. Reluctantly, David Morton signed on to a business venture in New York City. Joanna Morton fell seriously ill, and the remaining family sent the children to relatives. Buck and his brother John resided with cousins in Charlotte County after the death of their mother in April 1867, while three other brothers—Quin, Breckinridge, and David—all moved west to Lewisburg. His sister Joanna stayed with relatives in Washington, D.C. For several years, the scattered family existed in this unstable pattern. The weight became too heavy for David Morton, and within two years he suffered a mental breakdown in New York.[6]

The year 1869 changed Buck Morton's life. In May, the teenager attended political speeches from local candidates on the public square grounds accompanied by his two young Marshall cousins, Griffin and John, and a family friend named Fred Beal. At least one of the four boys brought a gun to the rally. Although any of the boys might have possessed a weapon, John Marshall was the likely candidate. A former soldier with plenty of experience with firearms, he carried that day due to family honor. The political speech was given by a former slave of the Marshall family, Joe Holmes. Since Reconstruction began in earnest, a few African-American freedmen pursued political opportunities. Unknowingly, Holmes stirred anger in Charlotte County when preparing his speech. False reports whispered that the former slave planned to speak on the subject of "miscegenation," a period term denoting the mixing of races. These reports, patently ridiculous on its face, were designed to undermine Holmes' speech and campaign. Most people agreed that political ambition was his real motive. Unfortunately, the rumors had taken full effect. As Holmes began his speech, a shot rang out from the group of four boys, and Joe Holmes fell dead.[7]

The Richmond papers reported the incident under the byline "HOMICIDE IN CHARLOTTE COUNTY." The claims within stretched the imagination. In one column, there were statements of an unnamed African-American man attacking an unnamed Marshall boy. Holmes, who recently attended a political convention, saw one of the Marshall boys fire and miss. In the attempt to interfere, another saw it as an opportunity and fired the fatal shot. In truth, any of the four boys could have killed Holmes. Further, it was erroneously reported they were arrested and held for questioning—they departed too quickly for that to hold true. Years later, Griffin's daughter wrote that both Marshall boys escaped soldiers on the scene. In looking back at the incident, Griffin denied assassinating Joe Holmes—the only one of the four who discussed it. Given his denial and the fact that Morton never discussed to establish a tough cowboy reputation, John Marshall remained the likely suspect.[8]

Judge Hunter Holmes Marshall, cousin of Buck Morton and recipient of his last letter. Mary Marshall Papers, Beinecke Library, Yale University. Courtesy of the Fleck Family.

Missouri

The murder of Joe Holmes necessitated that Buck Morton and the other boys leave the area before the authorities arrived. Judge Hunter Holmes Marshall, the father of Griffin and John, was on business in Richmond. Scared relatives packed and transported the boys to Pamplin, the closest train station on the Norfolk & Western Railroad. They traveled west to St. Louis, where Mrs. Marshall's brother lived. On May 29, 1869, Griffin Marshall wrote his sister that they contacted a man named Taylor. A study of family letters revealed that their maternal uncle, James Wilmer

Stith, married into the Taylor family. He was engaged, or at least invested, in the banking and mining businesses in the St. Louis area.[9]

My Dear Sister:

> You must really excuse me for not writing you sooner but I have been sick nearly ever since I have been here and the other part of the time I didn't feel like writing. I haven't had anything to do at all—we have been waiting for Mr. Taylor's son to come down here—but he has been sick and is now worse and probably never will be able to come. The old man said that he (his son) could get us better situations than anyone else and advised us to wait for him and of course as we were under his care we took his advice and are now waiting to see what is going to turn up. Mr. T. Sr went up to see about his son yesterday and we are expecting him back every day.
>
> Morgan is well and in pretty good spirits, but I am not in good spirits, I am getting tired doing nothing and paying board.
>
> This is the hardest country I ever saw; there isn't a tree of any consequence in two hundred miles of this place. One day it is as hot as five hundred and the next day you can't wrap up and keep comfortable–now today it is very hot.[10]

From this letter, written weeks after departure, several clues to their flight emerged. "Morgan" was Morton, as there was no one named Morgan in the family. Knowing full well that they remained fugitives, Griffin Marshall hid certain facts or names within the text of the letters. "Mr. Taylor" was James Stith's father-in-law, Simon Triplett Taylor. The land Griffin described fit that of Missouri.[11]

Another possibility of their flight pattern indicated that Buck Morton and the three other boys parted ways shortly after the escape. William Morton appeared in the 1870 Federal Census in Charlotte County, Virginia, but the tally was made in the latter part of the previous year. David Morton entrusted his cousin and employer, Samuel Pride Daniel, with Buck's care. In a January 1868 letter to his cousin Thomas Bouldin, the elder Morton stated Daniel's role as guardian.[12] In the letter, David Morton wrote, "I have made an engagement with Mr Saml Daniel and would be pleased to have you do what you can to sustain me in business— as soon as the Winter [sic] breaks up I wish to send Buck to school— Daniel gives me all I ask in the way of wages per month but cannot afford to continue such a salary unless I greatly increase his sales."[13]

There remained the possibility that Buck Morton revisited Virginia after his initial flight. The 1870 Federal Census for Charlotte County placed Buck, as "William Morton," in residence next to Daniel, housed with several domestic servants. Census statistics were gathered during the summer months, so Buck's presence may have been an extended visit. He worked as a clerk in his father's old dry goods store. Daniel appeared to have family residing just north of Springfield, Missouri. Given Buck's ties to Daniel, he could have stayed for a time.[14]

The Morton family's misfortunes continued after Buck cut many of his old ties to Virginia. On September 12, 1870, David Holmes Morton died in New York. He was buried in an unmarked pauper's grave. Word of his madness and death finally reached relatives after a matter of months. In January 1871, Meriam Fontaine Cabell wrote Thomas T. Bouldin that she just learned of David Morton's death, and then only by accident. In addition to being a fugitive, Buck Morton was an orphan. Aside from his siblings, there was little reason for Buck to return to Charlotte County.[15]

Excepting Griffin Marshall's remarks in his first letter home after he fled west, there is no other shaded reference to Buck Morton's presence in St. Louis. However, there was tangible information about their St. Louis relations. In the 1870 Census, Griffin's Uncle James Stith lived in the city of Corondelet, later incorporated into St. Louis. Although his then-occupation was officially listed as bank clerk, Stith found employment on a railroad. His wife, Fannie Taylor Stith, was a Virginian. The St. Louis Stith Family was large—four sons, two daughters, a sister-in-law, her child, and two servants. As several generations of the Stith family dabbled in politics in their ancestral Maryland home, James continued this tradition in

Missouri. He was elected to the state legislature as representative of St. Louis' First Ward in November 1872. The only noted report of his activity during his term was recorded in the *Sedalia Daily Democrat*—in January 1873. He sponsored a bill to regulate the level of compound interest on contracts.[16]

Both Buck Morton and his relatives followed a winding path over the next decade. Historians during the 1920s, notably Maurice Garland Fulton, sought answers to Buck's whereabouts. In 1928, he located Morton's sister, Joanna Hurxthal, through the court clerk in Greenbrier County, West Virginia.[17] They corresponded, and the notes kept by Fulton's contemporary Robert Mullin revealed Joanna's characterization of her brother. Buck was "perhaps wild and reckless, but brave, tender and generous...well educated for his age at leaving school."[18]

One of the few sources that linked Buck Morton to Springfield, Missouri was Roswell, New Mexico resident "Uncle Jim" Miller, who claimed that he and the Virginian had common acquaintances there. Miller traversed the same territory as Morton at the time. In 1869, Miller ran a blacksmith shop in northern Missouri, and the following year decided to strike out for Colorado. This coincided with Morton's travel in Missouri.[19]

Joanna Hurxthal wrote Maurice Fulton that her brother clerked in a Denver hotel when he first wrote them. Buck "sold his horse, gun and watch.... [H]e went first to Denver, from there we heard from him, he was clerking in a hotel."[20] A check of the 1874 Denver City Directory listed twenty hotel establishments. Among the popular inns were the American House, Grand Central, and Taylor's Hotel. Given that many prominent businessmen stayed in Denver, it was plausible that Jimmy Dolan or another cattle baron hired Morton while there. Denver newspapers during the period often published lists of prominent guests at its hotels. John Chisum stayed at the American Hotel in late February 1873, a hotel most of the cattle barons frequented. In December 1873, the American hosted both Texas cattleman John Hittson and New Mexico politician Stephen Elkins.[21]

The length of Buck Morton's Denver employment and subsequent move to New Mexico Territory was unknown, but there were plenty of opportunities. The Denver & Rio Grande Railway was then the only direct train route into the New Mexico Territory with daily departures by late 1873. Information from family letters trailed off, but historians pieced together a few of Morton's movements. Texas historian Ed Bartholomew, in his biography of outlaw Jessie Evans subtitled *A Texas Hide-Burner*, wrote that Buck drifted into Texas. He reportedly worked on ranches in McCulloch and Concho Counties before his employment by James Dolan in New Mexico Territory. Mullin wrote fellow researcher Phil Rasch that he suspected Bartholomew's book contained many errors, but did not specify his employment in Texas as one of them. He wrote, "To Bartholomew, whom I never met or corresponded with, I wrote a courtesous [sic] letter requesting authentication of 13 doubtful points in his JESSE EVANS. He replied in a reasonable and friendly manner; had misplaced some of his notes...."[22]

If Bartholomew found source material that proved Morton's presence in Texas, it never came to light. More probable was Morton's fleeting presence during various cattle drives across the state. The path of the Goodnight-Loving Trail passed through or near Concho and McCulloch Counties and terminated in the Pecos River Valley, an area familiar to Buck. Secondly, he must have gained adequate experience as a cowhand. Only an experienced herdsman or a trusted employee reached the level of a ranch foreman.

Regardless of how he ended up in the region, new adventures loomed for Buck. One suspicious account stated he worked the silver mines in the Arizona Territory. According to an unverified newspaper story authored by an enemy, Buck allegedly killed his mining partner in the mountains. Mullin was not convinced Morton committed this crime. Although an unlikely event, it was never proved nor disproved.[23]

Buck's brother Quin Morton received occasional letters from him. In February 1875, a relative disclosed that Quin was upset that Buck had sent him an unaddressed letter from "Mexico." This spiked fears about the fate of his brother, and it colored his moods. On one occasion, a relative described how Quin, after reading his brother's letter, had a fit and fell on the icy ground.[24] She wrote, "He [Quin] had had [sic] a very severe fall on the ice—& remained unconcious [sic] 12 hours-He went about town & insulted several of his friends. Finally some of his friends took him home & the physician was afraid his skull was fractured. He <u>Had</u> received a letter from Buck, who is in Mexico <u>&</u> He did not give his address. Which thing worried Quin very much-"[25]

Quin Morton, brother of Buck and later mine owner in West Virginia. Courtesy of Helen Payne and the Wilson Family.

Quin Morton had reason to worry, although he could not foretell the danger to his brother. In this early period, Buck was briefly Billy the Kid's boss. The working relationship between them soured quickly, but long enough to establish a sobriquet. George W. Coe related that while working at various ranches, Bonney became known as "El Chavito," or "The Kid." He came to the Pecos country looking for his old associate, Jessie Evans, who he met in La Mesilla, in the southwest corner of New Mexico Territory. The Kid found Morton, Baker, and Evans driving cattle to Lincoln and offered payment of five dollars a head, despite the few number of animals. The herd mysteriously increased on the way to Lincoln. When they got to town, Morton and Baker argued with him over the division of money. Ultimately, they refused to pay the Kid at all. Allegedly the Kid stated, "Well, you are just about the dirtiest bunch of curs I've ever met." Morton told him to clear out, which nearly caused a gunfight. Keep in mind that Coe was the Kid's steadfast ally and his account, like most descriptions from that side of the Lincoln County War, described Morton as a villain. Another version of the story, related by Lily Klasner, recounted that the Kid was personally "bawled out" by Buck for "some trivial offense" that triggered his temper.[26]

> [The Kid] spent a few days there at the Murphy-Dolan cow camp. Billy Morton was the boss there, and when the Kid returned in a short time to Seven Rivers, he told Will that Morton had given him a terrible bawling out for something or other and that he meant to get even with him. It was when he was smarting from this trouble with Billy Morton that he proposed to go along to Texas with us.... I think this difficulty with Billy Morton was the beginning of the implacable hatred the Kid showed for him, which culminated in Morton's death a few months later.[27]

Buck's job was another factor that led to his death. Chisum moved his lucrative herd of Texas longhorn cattle to a ranch near Roswell, New Mexico Territory. With a good water supply, the cattleman made an inspired choice of location. Dolan routed his own cattle to the Pecos, and bought some land near the budding settlement of Seven Rivers. His cow camp sprawled to the south of the town, near the Black River. Dolan shortly hired Buck Morton as his foreman.[28]

According to Alexander McSween's widow Susan, Morton sometimes crossed the line. She later wrote about the young foreman's brush with rustling.

> You have been told about Dolan moving his herd of cattle from off the Carrizozo Range to the lower edge of Mr. Chisums to increase his herd. Billy Morton was his Foreman in about a month after they were down there. John Chisum took a lot of cowboys went down and cut out about 40 head of cows with their brands on them he asked Billie "what do you mean by this." Billy responded "I thought I could get away with them." Some time after that Chisum moved his cattle north to the Canadian River.[29]

Again, Mrs. McSween, by then remarried, represented an "anti-house" viewpoint. To her, Morton's alleged attempt to steal cattle from Chisum was a business decision. Chisum, on the other hand, had minimal impact on the Kid's subsequent actions. Instead, it was the Kid's resentment over being cheated and fired by Morton that kindled his later actions.

Indeed, part of the problem was the expansive land partitioned between the two camps. North of Seven Rivers was a spring owned by a man named Blake. In 1877, Blake sold his property to "House" entrepreneur Lawrence Murphy, who sought local competition with John Chisum. Lincoln County resident Lily Klasner related that property changed hands, inevitably to Murphy. Allegedly, the land was purchased to poach from the rich Chisum herds. Even the brand was compromised, as rustlers added to the Chisum long rail symbol to Murphy's arrow with "tip and feathers."[30]

Chisum Cowboys at the South Spring Ranch. Courtesy of the Phillips Family.

Buck Morton was foreman of Dolan's cow camp near the Black River from the onset, and the itinerant cowboy life attracted a number of other familiar names. According to his letter, Buck was in Dolan's employ for a full twelve months—or March 1877. He knew the men that worked the ranches and later captured him. The ranch on the Feliz River owned by Tunstall employed McCloskey and Middleton. MacNab worked as a cattle detective for Hunter & Evans, a rival cattle outfit, prior to employment with Tunstall. "Big Jim" French wandered into New Mexico from the Indian Territory. According to Fulton's *History of the Lincoln County War*, several already nursed grudges against Dolan.[31]

If Morton rustled cattle, and there was every indication that he was involved in a minor capacity, he had the right group of people to do so. Frank Baker and Jessie Evans, both no strangers to illegal activity, passed their time at the Murphy-Dolan Ranch. Another cowhand, Dick Lloyd, belonged to a family that formerly resided in Lincoln, but resettled in the

Pecos Valley in 1873. Klasner described Lloyd as a dual personality. "He was a good-hearted, hard-working boy about whom it was told that he would drink too much mean whiskey. He liked to go to Lincoln, get good and drunk, then race up and down the street firing his six-shooter. He always shot into the air, and never tried to hurt anyone. So far as I know, Dick Lloyd never killed anyone or stole anything."[32]

Buck's money was another matter. Given the meager pay, it was little wonder if he turned to rustling to supplement his income. In 1954, Mullin examined Morton's earnings, and wrote Rasch that "he was supposed to receive $60.00 a month but Dolan owned [sic] him $600.00" and further pondered "that he was paid for only two of the twelve months he risked his neck for bro. Dolan."[33] According to Morton's final letter, he worked for Dolan twelve months—and specifically "since the 9th of March '77."[34]

If Morton's length of employment was at issue, so was the possibility he did not come to New Mexico Territory alone. Another hand who worked at the cow camp, Charles Marshall, could have been Griffin or John Marshall. This hypothesis was through a choice of alias. A brother of Griffin and John, Charles Marshall, resided in Virginia. County records located that sibling back east in February 1878. Griffin's daughter Margaret wrote years later that she believed the brothers went to Nevada, then on to Montana and Idaho. It was true that John Marshall, who established himself as a businessman in Montana, traversed this path. However, the space between Griffin's letters left much undocumented time.[35]

Seven Rivers, more a cluster of homes than an actual town, was sometimes known as "Dogtown" because of the profusion of prairie dogs. The budding village was founded by Virginians. Despite the hard country, the natural contour of the trail from the Texas Hill Country to the Pecos River necessitated the settlement. It attracted ranching families such as the Jones and Olingers. By reputation, the cowhands became famous as the "Seven Rivers Warriors."[36]

Buck Morton's strongest connection to Seven Rivers was his girlfriend, Helen "Rosalla" Beckwith. Phil Rasch, with fellow historian Lee Myers, in an article entitled "The Tragedy of the Beckwiths" in the

1963 *English Westerners Brand Book,* confirmed Buck had a romantic interest.[37] Helen was one of the daughters of Alabaman Hugh Beckwith and his Spanish-born wife, Refugia Pino. The relationship was known to various members of the family, including her younger sister, Laura Beckwith Oliver. Myers obtained a letter from a niece, which stated "Billy Morton was in charge of a cattle range—he was in love with Rosalle...."[38] Lily Klasner, or Sallie Chisum, whichever authored this particular account, stated that Morton was "cow boss" of all the Murphy Nolan [sic] cow camps. She noted him as a former resident of Richmond and that he "had a girl ... a beauty in every way...Called [sic] the "Bell" fo [sic] the Pecos Valley...."[39]

Laura Beckwith Oliver, sister of Buck Morton's romantic interest. Courtesy of Harold Beckwith.

According to Rasch, the Beckwith family arrived in New Mexico Territory in 1870, settling on a ranch north of Seven Rivers. The family ran afoul of Chisum, who believed the Beckwiths, among other area ranchers, rustled cattle belonging to him. In the spring of 1877, Chisum's men struck back. Neighbors warned Helen and one of her sisters to leave before trouble broke out, but they remained. The gun battle that followed was one of the principle conflicts in what was known as the Pecos War. Rasch wrote a group with Baker, Evans, and likely Morton, rode to save the Beckwiths. After some assurances, Chisum called off his men.[40]

A final highlight of Buck Morton's life as a camp foreman was the settlement of his estate, particularly his horse. On June 8, 1878, *The Mesilla News* ran an interesting article about the fate of the animal. Morton's horse was taken by his captors.

> The governor had official information that Copeland had sent a body of thirty armed men under a notorious assassin and outlaw as his deputy, to obtain a pony said to belong to the estate of the young man Morton, whom these same men had murdered while a prisoner in their hands.
>
> They rode 100 miles to lower Pecos and took 30 ponies (same number as in party) plus Mortons pony. Kidnapped a Navajo Indian and shot him. They were "administering to the Morton estate" and were asking to "administer to the Navajo's estate."
>
> The pony was to be sold by law, after deducting costs and expenses by Alexander McSween and he was to "administer to the Morton estate."[41]

Buck Morton's estate was inventoried by Lincoln County Administrator David Easton on July 8, 1879. It consisted of his mare and the amount due him by Dolan, $653-which he stated "I have not been able to collect."[42] The Lincoln County Probate Court Judge, Florencio Gonzales, ordered Easton to sell the sorrel mare. On September 6, 1880, Easton recorded an administrative statement. The horse was sold for $70 at private sale, but fees totaling $52.75 were subtracted, leaving a total of $17.25 as Morton's entire estate.[43]

According to Laura Beckwith Oliver, Buck desired the horse for his sweetheart Helen. She wrote as part of her memoir, later obtained by Lee Myers, "...before he died he told them to let Rosalle have his horse Billy—a beautiful bay horse—he also sent his watch and other relics to be sent to his sister in the East."[44] The relics disappeared and the horse never went to the intended recipient. Even in death, Buck Morton was unlucky.

3

TWO HIDDEN LIVES

Frank Baker, AKA Hart and William McCloskey

In relating the background of Buck Morton, there were plenty of motives that spurred Billy the Kid to kill him. In addition to fiery personalities that far exceeded the war for profits, romance was also a likely factor—as rumors persisted about the Kid's interest in Helen Beckwith. In assessing the motives for the murder of the other two victims in Blackwater Canyon, Frank Baker and William McCloskey, different answers emerged. The former took the Kid's place as Jessie Evans' sidekick, while the latter was regarded with constant suspicion. Unlike Morton, Baker was never close to the Kid. McCloskey was murdered by others, but certainly the Kid shared their suspicions.

There were few figures in the Lincoln County War harder to describe than Frank Baker and William McCloskey. Both left sketchy trails behind them, with only hints to their pasts. Unlike Morton, who used his real name, Baker was an alias. Alternative names were often used to divert shame from the family name or to simply avoid the law. In Baker's case, both were probably true. McCloskey, older and with little to hide, was not an alias. Even after a careful study of their backgrounds, few answers find solid ground.

Descriptions of Baker were often unfavorable. The fullest description came from Ash Upson. He was "about 22," and cowardly, as he shot his enemies in the back. However, Upson was hardly a neutral critic. A truncated version of a letter he wrote to his niece Florence Downs Muzzy was summarized in Maurice G. Fulton's book, *Roswell in its Early Years.*[1]

This fellow Frank Baker, has shot innocent men when they were on their knees, pleading for life. With [a] brutal laugh had held a pistol to their heads, and after blowing their brains out, kicking the inanimate body and face to jelly. His countenance was the strongest argument that could be produced in favor of the Darwinian theory. Brutish in feature and expression, he looked a veritable gorilla. He boasts that his father killed 18 men before he was hung in Texas, and that his three brothers had killed a half dozen, more or less, each before they were killed. That even his mother had killed a deputy sheriff in Texas. That he was 22 years of age the last of the family and had killed 13 men and wanted twenty before he was 25 years old. I have often heard of the family. Their names are Hart not Baker.[2]

The full unpublished letter from Upson to his niece was even more scathing. It was clear that the former newspaper man loathed Baker. Far more than the capsule version in *Roswell in its Early Years*, he dedicated several full paragraphs to the effort.

I have, now, nothing of importance to write. My mind is full, to-day, of a horrible sight I witnessed day before yesterday. The body of the very worst, most beastly murderer this country ever saw, dead, and mutilated in a most shocking manner. It would be treason to say I am sorry he is killed, but really I have enough Christian charity not to gloat or even rejoice over any man's death.

This fellow, Frank Baker, has shot innocent men when they were on their knees, pleading for life. With brutal laugh held a pistol to their heads, and after blowing their brains out, kicking the inanimate body and face to a jelly. His countenance was the strongest argument that could be produced in favor of the Darwinian theory. Brutish in feature and expression, he looked a veritable gorilla. He boasts that his father killed 18 men before he was hung in Texas, and that his 3 brothers had killed a half-dozen, more or less each, before they were killed, that even his mother had killed a deputy sheriff in Texas. That he was 22 years of age, the last of the family and had killed 13 men, and wanted 20 before he was 25 years old. I have often heard of the family. Their names are Hart not Baker. They had no friends and no companions, even amongst the vilest outlaws, except companions compelled by fear. They were a fearful curse to whatever section they went. Birds of ill-omen. They none of them knew the taste of fear. Would look into the barrel of a rifle as unconcernedly as they would gaze at a rising sun. This one died cursing the officers who were forced to kill after arresting him. He was a daring brute.

"The race of whom 'twas said that, where they trod, Never grass grew again; The valiant but all-blighting foes of men."

What an epitaph; and as I looked I shuddered at what, should the orthodox theory be true, was now now [sic] his fate for eternity.[3]

An analysis of Upson's letter brought forth more questions than answers. The fact that Upson used so much ink describing Baker indicated he knew him better than simple association. The postmaster wrote in great detail on the murder, odd for someone who never witnessed the tragedy. Although highly emotional, Tunstall was mentioned nowhere in these paragraphs. Secondly, Upson was one of the few sources who knew Baker's real name was Hart.

The Hart surname, as it pertained to outlawry in the New Mexico Territory, surfaced half a decade before Frank Baker's death. Among the late Phil Rasch's journal articles was one entitled "The Horrell War," originally published in the July 1956 *New Mexico Historical Review*. In 1873, the Horrells arrived in Lincoln from Lampasas County, Texas, northwest of Austin. A great deal of animosity developed between the local Spanish-speaking families and the Horrells. The result was an escalating series of retaliatory strikes. Before long, thirteen people were dead. In December, the Horrells and their allies attacked a Mexican freighter. Among their associates named in the warrants from that attack was one Edward "Little" Hart.[4]

Historians pondered over the Horrell connection for decades. They recounted the family's westward movement from Arkansas to Lampasas, to unexpected tribal incursions in New Mexico Territory. Rasch noted all five Horrell brothers—Ben, Martin, Merritt, Sam, and Thomas—were "high strung." In 1869, the Horrells visited New Mexico Territory and paid a heavy price for it. The patriarch of the family was killed in a tribal raid, and the rest of the family returned to Texas. After the violent death of Lampasas Sheriff Shadrach T. Denson on January 14, 1873, they moved back into New Mexico Territory. A gun battle in the Lampasas town square between the Horrells and their allies against the lawmen resulted in several deaths and arrests. They fled after local townspeople freed them. The arrival of the Horrells in Lincoln County was chronicled by writer Emerson Hough, in 1907's _The Story of the Outlaw._ Hough wrote that the ranches they purchased on the Ruidoso River were "staked" by Major Lawrence Murphy. Any ranch of this magnitude needed the support of the "House."[5]

The Hart-Horrell connection dangled on sparse accounts. Any evidence connecting Edward Hart to Frank Baker remained flimsy, although a couple of clues were provided by Klasner. In one account, she related Edward Hart's killing of Joe Haskins at Picacho in late 1873 or early 1874. The description provided noted Hart was small in stature and had a "sandy complexion." He grew impatient with his neighbors over a tardy breakfast, and while stewing he inquired about the residents of a nearby home. Hart was told that Haskins and his Mexican wife lived there. This angered him, as he apparently disapproved of marriages between Mexicans and Anglos. Hart stormed to the Haskins home, opened the door, and shot the husband. In a separate account in her book, Klasner described Baker by name. From these two accounts, she knew both Baker and Hart—always separating the two. By her account they were not the same person. The only other explanation is that Sallie Chisum really authored the segment on Baker.[6]

The nature of the Baker-Hart connection puzzled most historians.

Some assumed that Baker was "Little" Hart based on the identification provided in Ash Upson's letter. The truth was that no one really knew. In Mullin's notes, he doubted they were the same person and referred to the confusion surrounding the death of a man named Hart at the hands of John Selman, the shady Texan who drifted between law enforcement and criminal activity.[7] Mullin wrote Rasch in December 1955, "You didn't tell me what it is that may connect Frank Baker and Hart. I suppose that is Little Hart who killed a buddy because the later [sic]married a Mexican, in January '74. It would be interesting to know if Little Hart turned up again under the name Baker in the Lincoln County War."[8]

Baker's counterparts provided little assistance to his origin. Jessie Evans, a shady character always on the cutting edge of banditry, was in the New Mexico Territory when the Horrell War began. Although Baker and Evans traveled together regularly by 1876, they met through Texas cattle drives, or another common friend, John Kinney. That year they frequented La Mesilla, a center of commerce in the Territory, and the city of El Paso, located on the western edge of Texas. Baker's movements with these associates revealed little of his past.[9]

One consistent connection provided was Hart's possible origins in Texas. Numerous families with the surname were found across the state. A prominent Hart family resided in El Paso, as Simeon Hart owned a mill in the town's earliest days. Maurice Fulton researched this particular Hart family to ascertain if Frank Baker belonged to them. However, there were notable digressions from Upson's description of the family. Simeon Hart's death in 1874 was peaceful, not violent. Other Texans with the Hart surname lacked Upson's claim of a string of violent deaths. Therefore, other parts of the state bared attention.[10]

Another hint to Baker's real identity was found as an innocent piece of another account of Billy the Kid. A history buff named Frazier Hunt wrote _The Tragic Days of Billy the Kid_ in 1956, a year after the death of Colonel Fulton. Hunt credited Fulton with information furnished in his book. Within it, he described Baker as "part Cherokee." There was a contingent of the Regulators from the so-called Indian Territory, represented by Fred Waite, who was part Chickasaw, and Jim French. If Hunt was correct in his description of Baker, and he was indeed part Cherokee, his regional origins narrowed to Arkansas, Indian Territory, Missouri and parts of central Texas.[11]

Given these new geographic bearings, two other Hart families emerged. One Hart family resided in central Texas, close to Lampasas. In 1845, Aaron H. Hart, a Tennessee man of partial Cherokee descent, married Caroline Gentry in Mississippi. They migrated to Texas in the late 1840s. An experienced cowboy, Aaron's job and family grew. By the 1860 Federal Census, he had four children. Tragically, he died in Callahan County, Texas, in the summer of 1867, aged forty-one. After his death, his family built a new residence, and employed a contemporary of outlaw Sam Bass as their carpenter. Caroline lived until 1881, but it was unknown if she ever shot a lawman. She was good with a gun, as she fired on attacking Comanche tribesmen on their ranch. However, notable discrepancies appeared when compared to Upson's description of the family. For example, the 1880 Federal Census for Callahan County, Texas clearly described four living sons of the couple. Still, connections to the Cherokee and the cattle trade corroborated Baker's background, as did Aaron's early death. A man named Benjamin Franklin Baker resided nearby—providing a possible alias. When the death and subsequent estate settlement of this gentleman occurred in 1863, Aaron Hart was agent for the rent of the house Baker resided. If the outlaw Frank Baker were in this family, he would have known Benjamin Franklin Baker. It made the Aaron Hart family an intriguing possibility as the kin of outlaw Frank Baker.[12]

One account with the connections of the Aaron Hart family was written by W.W. Hunter of Coleman County, Texas. This account was featured in local historian Beatrice Grady Gay's book *Into the Setting Sun*. Hunter was one of Coleman County's oldest living residents and remembered the children of Aaron Hart. He related the following account of son James.

Mr. Jim Hart had a ranch about 15 miles to the north of us in Callahan County. One day Mr. Hart was away from home. His wife and two other women were at home, also his brother John. A party of about 40 Indians raided the ranch. They most always came in the daytime to raid the homes of the settlers, because the men were more likely to be away. The Indians got within about two hundred yards of the house before they were discovered. John Hart shot into them and beat them back about a hundred yards. One Indian being very brave did not stop, but kept coming on, Mr. Hart shooting at him all the time. When he was near enough to be seen well, they saw that he had a buffalo mop and horns on his head. He stopped, shook his head and bellowed like a buffalo. The other Indians kept shouting to him, and he turned back and ran towards them. As he ran Mr. Hart shot him in the back of the head and he fell off his horse, dead…

The Harts had plenty of guns and ammunition, as Mr. Hart had recently returned from Mexico and brought with him six or eight Winchester rifles. As fast as John Hart emptied one during the fight the women had another loaded and ready for him.[13]

The research on this particular Hart family revealed no direct proof of Frank Baker's identity, but interesting reasons to hide his name. Aaron Hart was half-brother to prominent cattle stockman John Hittson, who knew and employed cowboys. Some of these same men worked in the New Mexico Territory. In 1872, a mixed herd of Hart and Hittson cattle ended up near Chisum's ranch at South Spring. There were enough clues that created the possibility that Hart "AKA" Frank Baker knew the area through this family.[14]

Further information, or disinformation, clouded the positive identification of Frank Baker. A Navajo named Juan Armijo killed Regulator Frank MacNab, one of the assailants in Blackwater Canyon. By Armijo's own admission, the death occurred at the request of a relative of Frank

Baker who lived near Seven Rivers. This relative was known as Robert Baker. When Armijo was in turn captured at his home and summarily executed, he related Robert Baker's role in the MacNab slaying to one of his captors, Francisco Trujillo.

> When Atanasio Martinez, John Scroggin, Billy the Kid and I arrived at the door of the hut, Juan Armijo spoke up and said "How are you Kiko [Trujillo]?" "Come on out" I said to Juan. "You have killed Macky Nane [MacNab]" to which he nodded in assent but adding that it was by order of Robert Baker under threat of being prosecuted himself, should he fail to carry out instructions. I then made my way to Macky Nane [MacNab] who had been hiding behind some tree trunks in an effort to defend himself against those who were shooting at the house, and killed him.[15]

This account assumed the Baker name was actually an alias, but there was a family of that name who arrived in Seven Rivers years later. This group of Bakers came from Texas, but they were not related.[16]

Frank Baker was seen in Mesilla as early as 1875. Throughout the following year, he was mentioned for shady deeds attributed to him. _The Mesilla Independent_ reported in July 1877 that warrants were issued for John Kinney, Jessie Evans, and Frank Baker. By then Kinney established himself as an outlaw after he and others—which included Evans, Jim McDaniels, and perhaps Baker—shot out the windows of a dance hall during a New Year's Eve event. Two soldiers and a citizen died.[17]

By 1876, Baker was a seasoned herdsman working for Chisum. Some described him favorably during this early period. For example, Gus Gildea, a fellow cowboy, wrote Maurice Fulton a kinder portrait of Baker.

> When I knew Baker in 1876 on the trail with steer cattle from Pecos river, N.M. to Sulphur Springs valley, Ariz., he was a very amiable young man; kind hearted, generous and of a jolly disposition, far different in every particular to what you have him quoted.

We parted near Fort Bowie, Ariz. in Nov, 1876 and never again met, that I know of, 'though I occasionally heard of him as a participant in the War activities <u>versus</u> the Chisum forces but I am not cognizant of the facts that led him to join the opposeing [sic] party, unless it was the arrogance of Chisum, for I considered Baker a square, brave man in every respect, though he could have changed, but I doubt it, minus proof.[18]

Lily Klasner, or Sallie Chisum, described Baker with kindness, and provided more clues to his identity.

Because Frank Baker was suspected of having a part in the killing of Tunstall I must say that I think that rumor a misrepresentation. I knew him a long time. He was from a good family in Syracuse, New York. Shortly after we came to the Hondo, Frank Baker, who was working for Uncle John Chisum, came through with a herd of cattle en route to San Carlos, Arizona, and stopped at our place. When on my way to the store, I met a cowboy who noticed a cheap ring I was wearing and said, "Little girl, let me see that." I handed it to him with the expectation that he would return it; instead he put it on his little finger and said he would keep it. He had been drinking and scarcely knew what he was doing. I ran toward the house crying; I was only about nine years old.

Frank Baker asked why I was crying and I told him, adding that I was afraid I would not get my ring back. Frank said, "Don't cry, Little Girl; I'll get it for you." Later in the day he brought the ring which he had taken from the sleeping man's finger. He asked for a bucket of water and I watched him pour it slowly over the head of the man who had taken the ring.

I knew, too, that Uncle John thought well of Baker. I never heard of his having stolen anything or killed anybody. Perhaps after he went to work for the Murphy-Dolan crowd he suffered the corruption of character that characterized that outfit. But so long as he was with Uncle John he conformed to Uncle John's standards which prohibited stealing or killing.[19]

Klasner—or perhaps Sallie Chisum—wrote of Baker's character exactly opposite to the brash cowboy that Upson described. As with Morton, Baker was tempered by circumstance. He dealt harshly with herdsmen and kindly with others. Nonetheless, his background was more violent than Morton's own, and while Buck was not known as an outlaw, Baker was.

Whichever image fit him, Baker allied himself with Kinney and Jessie Evans. The collective group became known as "The Boys." They stole at will and evaded a sheriff's deputy sent to arrest them. Evans included other drifting cowhands such as Baker and Morton in their exploits in Dona Ana County. In July 1877, a manhunt ensued for the marauding "Boys," but the group disappeared toward El Paso. The disappearance was brief, as that month an embarrassing newspaper story appeared in the *Mesilla Valley Independent* and reported that Evans, Baker, and associate Nicholas Provencio were arrested, suspected of filibustering in Mexico. This trumped-up charge meant they unduly attempted to interfere with the sovereignty of that country—something this group had little chance of achieving. Albert Jennings Fountain, politician and editor of the *Mesilla Valley Independent,* published a detailed account. All three suspects rode under assumed names. Mariano Baltier was the alias for Provencio; Baker used the name Frank Johnson; and Jesse Evans rode as Jesse Williams. Two other names in the article, unknown compatriots, were Charles Williams and "M. Jones." Provencio rode a stolen horse from a Mesilla resident, which led to their identification. On the evening of July 8, they rode armed three miles into Mexico. Although they took the precaution of notifying authorities in El Paso of their peaceful intentions, Mexican authorities worried. They were arrested the following morning, but after a few days of hard labor in Mexico, U.S. Commercial Agent Solomon C. Schutz secured their release and return of their property—with the exception of Provencio's stolen horse. Fountain's editorial netted no subsequent arrest. The "Boys" slipped away and reappeared in Lincoln County.[20]

By autumn, William Bonney met John Tunstall. The aforementioned argument with Baker and Morton over money on their common cattle drive led to a rift with the entire Murphy-Dolan concern. The Kid returned to tell his former workers. Miguel Otero wrote that his "statement was received in ominous silence. For a time, it looked as if the interview might come to a bloody ending, but angry expostulations, eager arguments, and impassioned entreaties all failed to shake his determination."[21] Jessie Evans took the bragging in stride, but Baker wanted to fight Bonney. The Kid allegedly baited him, but did not get the desired battle. "Yes, you damned dog – right now, when you're nine to one. Come on, Baker. You're stinking for a fight. You never killed a man you didn't shoot in the back. Come out here and fight like a man."[22]

The statement in Otero's book highlighted the personal bitterness between them. It was about his treatment by Baker and Morton—a personal motive, and not about Tunstall's right to ranch. As with Morton, Baker personified a cheat.

While doing their handiwork in Lincoln County, the "Boys" found more trouble. They stole horses and pack mules from the Mescalero Apaches and mill-owner Doctor Almer N. Blazer, according to the report by U.S. Indian Agent Frederick Godfroy. The "Boys" relieved Dick Brewer's ranch of four horses in September. Seven members, including Baker, were caught with a stolen horse in hand. Brewer rode out, accompanied by fellow hands Charlie Bowdre and Josiah "Doc" Scurlock, but found themselves outnumbered by the "Boys," so they returned to Brewer's ranch empty-handed. For this action, three more of the assailants in Blackwater Canyon had personal grudges against Baker.[23]

The "Boys" continued their criminal activity in Lincoln County well into October 1877, but afterward slipped back to Mesilla. A passing traveler saw nine men, all members of the "Boys," rob a stagecoach near Fort Cummings. In addition, the group made off with several horses from a coal camp in the Burro Mountains. After yet another theft a few days

later, a six-man posse was formed to capture them. The lawmen found
their quarry, but shortly realized they were outnumbered and retreated
after a gunfight near the village of Santa Barbara.[24]

However, the "Boys" got sloppy. Arriving in the town of Tularosa
in late October, they drank down a portion of the spirits in the town's
saloon. In their drunken revelry, they fired aimlessly into the walls of the
canteen as they rode out of town. The gang proceeded on their drunken
rampage and shot up the property of a man named Sylvester, a former
witness against Evans. Robert Mullin described the actions through an
article in the *Mesilla Independent* on October 13, 1877. The article noted
that "Sylvestre" was a first name, and he begged them to spare his sick
children. The hapless victim received laughter for his pleas, but his request
was granted. His pet dog was not so fortunate. Law enforcement arrived
in force, and the group fled.[25]

The column in the *Mesilla Independent* emphasized Baker's status in
the organization. A pro-"Boys" letter to the editor, authored by a member
or sympathizer of the "Boys," knew that newsprint was an effective tool
for manipulating public opinion. The letter, entitled "GRAND REUNION
OF "THE BOYS," was signed by the pseudonym "Fence Rail." The
"resolutions" sent forth jabbed at Fountain, the ardent foe of the "Boys."
Baker was ranked as "captain" in a mock military jibe.[26] "This business was
concluded with the following result. Captain Jesse Evans was promoted
to the colonel. Nick Provencio and Frank Baker, on account of their
proficiency in horse stealing, etc. were elected captains, and all the balance
of the band were made captain by brevet...."[27] In addition, "Fence Rail"
mentioned Baker a second time. The mocking letter read that "resolutions
having been adopted Captain Nicholas Provencio produced a copy of the
Independent, a huge fire was built, and the obnoxious paper was thrown
into the flames. The gang, headed by Captain Evans, now marched around
the pyre to the inspiring strains of the "Rogues' March" performed by
Captain Baker on a fine tooth comb."[28]

Other than pointing out Baker's figurative musical ability, these
columns revealed the callous nature of the "Boys." They stole provisions

a second time from the Mescalero Indian Agency, but the act ended the series of raids there. Baker and Evans, along with George Davis, suspected to be Evans' brother, and compatriot Tom Hill, rode back to Seven Rivers. They fancied themselves safe there, but never counted on the tenacity of Dick Brewer. He, backed by Tunstall and McSween, secured the necessary warrants and posse under Sheriff William Brady. With fifteen men, they arrived at Hugh Beckwith's ranch, where the men holed up, and arrested them after a short gunfight on October 17th.[29]

Fountain's *Mesilla Independent* published several letters after this incident. One was penned by a gentleman named "D.H. Ewing" on October 20, 1877. Mullin doubted this was his or her real name, and the identity of the author narrowed to those residing in Lincoln. The content of the letter complimented Sheriff Brady for the capture.[30]

> About 2 o'clock this afternoon, Sheriff Brady and posse came into town having in their possession Jesse Evans, Frank Baker, Tom Hill and George Davis. They were followed and arrested after a feeble resistance early on the 17th day of October at Beckwith's ranch, Seven Rivers, New Mexico...As chief, all hail to our noble and deserving Sheriff Brady. We are proud of that noble and self-sacrificing posse (all residents of our renowned county) who so cheerfully followed and ventured with the determined leader.... The *chiefs of that band* are now lodged securely in the new jail at this place. And, we trust, being now cared for by the law's course will be permitted to go to its finality.[31]

Baker and Evans again found themselves in jail. The "new $3,000 jail," equivalent to about $60,000 in 1955, was built by Vermont-born George "Dad" Peppin, later a Lincoln County sheriff himself. Constructed partially underground, the jail was hardly "escape-proof," as Mullin quipped to Phil Rasch. A second letter sent to Fountain at the *Independent* revealed the infamous prisoners were "playing cards in the dungeon." They were loud but "brave," wrote the writer who signed himself as "Order."[32]

The divided nature of local sympathies contributed to the escape of the prisoners. Tunstall visited Baker and his cohorts while in the jail, poking them with taunts or jokes. According to historian Frederick Nolan, it was the "Boys" that invited him to visit. In either case, it appeared to be good-natured ribbing. Tunstall enjoyed his visit and sent for a bottle of whiskey. In the *Life and Death of John Henry Tunstall*, Nolan wrote that Brewer visited the prisoners as well. In the first few weeks of November 1877, the lax nature of the guards allowed the four prisoners an opportunity to escape. According to Mullin, Sheriff Brady replaced seven guards with one man, Iueillo Archulette. Soon after, a murderer named Katarino Romero walked out with "one or more other prisoners." Evans was said to be among the escapees.[33]

According to the *Life and Death of John Henry Tunstall*, the "Boys" rode out to Dick Brewer's ranch and bragged about their escape to local citizens. They told Brewer's cowhands that ten of them held a pistol to the jailer, knocked their shackles off with large rocks, and unhurriedly left Lincoln. In all likelihood, Tunstall knew less about the escape than he should have. Regardless which version of the escape was correct, Brady and Tunstall fell out over the matter, each upset at the actions of the other.[34]

Anger in the press spiked again in December 1877. Letters to the editor assessed blame for the escape. On December 3, 1877, a writer calling himself "Lincoln," probably an alias for Fountain or McSween, indicated the escape was engineered by "Pasha Boyle," a resident of the Pecos region. "Lincoln" took a swipe at Brady as well, writing, "P.S. After the escape the cells were found to be liberally supplied with files, knives, and augers, as also cotton sacks with rocks weighing from ten to twenty pounds. How's that for vigilance?"[35]

Aside from the bitterness found in newspaper columns in late 1877, the "Boys" vacated Lincoln County for newer horizons. A Missouri businessman named Charles Howard saw profits in the large salt beds near El Paso. The Mexican residents of the area became upset over the seizure of free salt that lasted for generations. Tension became violent, and Howard and two others were murdered. Kinney rode to El Paso with twenty-four New Mexicans, including Baker. In mid-December, with the permission of the Texas governor, El Paso Sheriff Charles Kerber incorporated the group into his posse. Colonel Edward Hatch, a well-known veteran of the Civil War, had overall command of soldiers, Kerber's men and a contingent of Texas Rangers. They took two prisoners who mysteriously died shortly after their capture. Fountain reported in the December 29, 1877 *Mesilla Independent* that the New Mexicans captured the two, and further intimated that Kinney engineered their execution. Colonel Hatch was said to be outraged, assessing the action as murder. Shortly after this bloody episode, on or about New Years Day, 1878, Kinney and Baker parted ways. From then until his death, Baker remained near the Pecos. Susan Barber, the widow of lawyer McSween, denied Billy the Kid associated with Baker and further doubted any association with Jessie Evans. However, the opposite was obviously true.[36]

Others mentioned Frank Baker in error. In Walter Noble Burns' *Saga of Billy the Kid* and later in Coe's book, *Frontier Fighter*, there was a direct reference to "Baker's sweetheart," Lizzie Lester. The excerpt read in the latter book, "... next morning young Baker gave me a bunch of keepsakes including a pretty gold watch, and requested me to send them to his sweetheart, Miss Lizzie Lester, in Syracuse, New York if anything happened to him."[37] Sallie Chisum Robert maintained a correspondence with Lizzie Lester for years. While Lizzie's family moved westward from Syracuse in 1872, they settled in Kansas.

Her father Henry, known as "Judge" Lester, settled in Hamilton County and founded the town of Syracuse the next year. At sixteen, she married Ed Davis and raised a son. As a hobby, Lizzie wrote articles under the pseudonym "Bramblebush," which she submitted to the Syracuse, New York newspapers. She divorced Davis, and later remarried John Durfee. She lived in Lake City, Kansas until her death on May 12, 1938.[38]

The problem with the account presented by Burns and Coe—it was the wrong Frank. In the course of the search for facts on Lizzie Lester, a historical mistake was uncovered. She was **not** the sweetheart of Frank

Baker! A letter proved Lizzie Lester's sweetheart was **Frank MacNab, not Frank Baker**. MacNab knew he was a hunted man after the murders of the three men in Blackwater Canyon, but the death of Sheriff Brady on April 1st sealed his fate. He gave the items to Sallie Chisum at that time. MacNab was killed on April 29th, and the letter penned from the South Spring Ranch on April 19th —only a day removed from the indictments of William Bonney, John Middleton, and Henry Brown for the murder of Sheriff Brady by a grand jury.[39]

> South Spring River
> Apr 19/4/78
>
> Miss Lizzie Lester
> Syracuse
> Kansas
>
> Dear Lizzie when you peruse these few lines and learn of the death of one who, held you in the highest esteem I hope the memory of pastfriendship will help to ameliorate the hard feelings that found existence between us. And convince you kindly towards one who has tried "at all times" to do right.
>   how [sic] much better for both of us it would have been had you understood me better, and listened to me, but that is of the past, and probably we are both to blame[.]
>   May your future be as bright as I would wish it is the last sentiments of your
>
> Very sincere friend
> Frank Macnab[40]

From this letter, it was clear that MacNab was the person who handed the letter to Sallie Chisum along with the keepsakes, and not Frank Baker. Further confirmation was found in a letter MacNab wrote to the editor of the *Dodge City Times* in July 1877—from Syracuse, Kansas. In the July 7, 1877 issue, the cattle detective objected to charges that he murdered two brothers named Casner in the Texas Panhandle the previous winter.[41]

Kansas resident Lizzie Lester Durfee and husband John in old age. She was incorrectly presumed to be the love of Frank Baker. She was Frank MacNab's romantic interest. Courtesy of Ron Cooke.

William McCloskey: Non-Violent Drifter

The third dead man at Blackwater Draw, William McCloskey, had a background as mysterious as Frank Baker. Ed Bartholomew, in his biography on outlaw Jessie Evans, wrote: "Old Man McClosky [sic], who tried to protect the Kid's prisoners Baker and Morton, only to die himself in the attempt, was a respected cattleman from DeWitt County, it was said."[42] Despite a search, no William McCloskey surfaced in DeWitt County during this time period. Lily Klasner assigned him an ethnic identity. She called him "a very good honest old scotchman who tried to save the lives of thes [sic] poor boys...."[43] His name had Scotch-Irish origins, but there was little evidence he was a first generation immigrant. As with Baker, McCloskey's origins were a guessing game, but with several distinct possibilities. A William McCloskey lived in New Mexico Territory long before the Lincoln County War. The 1870 Federal Census for Valencia County listed William McCloskey, aged 23, residing in the village of Peralta with wife Juana, sons Juan and Modesto, and a boarder named Simon Casias. He nor his family appear in the 1880 Federal Census. This William McCloskey was born in Kentucky, but hardly fit the description of "Old Man McCloskey." This assumed that he was 31 years of age at death. The greatest possibility of the real McCloskey lived outside both New Mexico Territory and Texas until shortly before the murders. In the 1860 Federal Census, William McCloskey, age thirty, appeared in the town of Troy, Kansas. He and his wife Sarah settled there from their Pennsylvania birthplaces. Sarah, without William, later reappeared in San Juan County, New Mexico Territory. This would have made him an "old man" of 48 years of age in 1878. His widow passed in the 1920s, and McCloskey's daughter married into a family interested in the silver mines of western Colorado. A brother, Edward, worked most of his life in Denver but later joined the family late in San Juan County. This William H. McCloskey remained a very good possibility.[44]

     The verified facts about McCloskey's life lay scattered in the records. He was a roving cowhand in the summer of 1875 when, under the name "William H. McCloskey," was a witness in a court case against the U.S. Indian Agent of the Mescalero Apache Agency, W.D. Crothers. It was indicative of how the "House" did business. At Lawrence Murphy's saloon in Lincoln, several members planned attacks against peaceful members of the Mescalero tribe. Crothers learned of the plans, and he refused to sign bills submitted by the "House." He was arrested on charges of larceny.

In the proceedings, McCloskey and fellow associate Sam Smith testified. Despite some friendly witnesses, Crothers was replaced as agent.[45]

In 1876, McCloskey briefly served as a special deputy sheriff. This came by way of a February 12, 1876 article in the *Mesilla News*. A gang of Mexican cattle rustlers posted stolen horses near Fort Stanton. Soldiers from the 9th Cavalry, accompanied by six men, including McCloskey, went after them. He received little more than mention, and then his name was misspelled.[46]

McCloskey drifted between ranches for the next year, although he found steady work with Tunstall. He was considered a temporary employee at the time. Walter Noble Burns, in *The Saga of Billy the Kid*, called him an "old buffalo hunter." Brewer's confidence faded when he worked for Tunstall because of his previous employment with the "House."[47]

Today, there are only questions on William H. McCloskey's background. Given these circumstances, McCloskey was an unlikely victim at Blackwater Draw. However, he was a vagabond with no set loyalties to either side. Brewer, and likely the Kid, did not trust him on the basis of his friendship with Morton. McCloskey's death was one of paranoia, not of greed.

Home of *Mesilla Independent* editor and politician Albert J. Fountain near Las Cruces, New Mexico. Author's Collections.

4

THE TUNSTALL MURDER WHODUNIT

Tradition and reality conflicted with the escalation of the Lincoln County War. The murder of the three men at Blackwater Draw received much press, but many viewed the action as retaliation for the death of British-born John Henry Tunstall. The series of retaliatory skirmishes led to action by official Washington. Frank Warner Angel, a New York jurist sent by the Justice and State Departments to sort out the facts, found his deponents on the defensive, even opinionated. James Dolan and several other witnesses in the Angel Report heightened the sensitivity. From a policeman's perspective, there was much denial of responsibility in the deed. Therefore, the depositions in the Angel Report were suspect on the truth.

The truth was something else entirely. The Mescalero Apache Reservation was founded in the spring of 1873. The newly-established boundaries confined a wandering people. They distrusted most of the cowboys surrounding them, and were bullied into accepting near-military rule. One outsider they trusted was Doctor Joseph H. Blazer, the owner of a nearby mill. They often traded with the residents of Tularosa, but their livelihoods were at the mercy of the U.S. Indian Agent. The home of the agent, originally in Fort Stanton, moved to Blazer's Mill in 1875.[1]

As the agent's office developed, the rules changed to meet the needs of the settlers- particularly on the subject of beef contracts. The official rationed cattle for food, and the plight of the agency favored the "House." One Mescalero remarked to Eve Ball, "At first we kill the cattle ourselves. Then they have a white man kill the cattle, cut up the meat and we go to the issue house and get beef."[2]

On July 30, 1877, a check signed by lawyer Alexander McSween for $1,545.13 to Lincoln Sheriff William Brady created a power struggle between the two competing cattle interests. Both had ties to the profitable contracts with the Mescalero Agency. A battle for cattle contracts with the Mescalero Apaches started between established ranchers supported by the so-called "Santa Fe Ring" and relative newcomers like Chisum. Tunstall localized the problem as one of the newcomers. Dolan and Murphy probably dismissed Tunstall as an easy mark in his early months. The Englishman knew little about the trade, but his enemies underestimated both Tunstall and his allies, and it all started with the check.[3]

On January 18, 1878, a letter to the *Mesilla Independent* appeared, penned by Tunstall and entitled "A Tax-Payer's Complaint." A quote, reportedly from Governor Axtell and underneath the dateline stated, "The present Sheriff of Lincoln County has paid nothing during his present term of office." It was a complaint about Lincoln County Sheriff William Brady, specifically talking about his collection of a check.

> ...Major Brady, as the records of this County show, collected over Twenty-five hundred dollars, Territorial funds. Of this sum Alex. A. McSween Esq., of this place, paid him over Fifteen hundred dollars by cheque on the First National Bank of Santa Fe, August 23, 1877.
>
> Said cheque was presented for payment by John H. Riley, Esq., of the firm of J.J. Dolan & Co, this last amount was paid by the last named gentleman to Underwood and Nash for cattle. Thus passed away over Fifteen hundred dollars belonging to the Territory of New Mexico.
>
> With the exception of thirty-nine dollars, all the taxes of Lincoln County for 1877 were promptly paid.... A delinquent tax-payer is bad; a delinquent tax collector is worse.
>
> J.H.T.[4]

Tunstall believed the "House," through Sheriff Brady, intended to run him out. By issuing his message through the newspaper, Tunstall hoped to repulse them. Instead, the public statement launched an immediate response by Dolan. The next week, an "Answer to Tax-payer's Complaint" was published in the same manner.

> Dear Sir—In answer to a communication in reference to taxpayers of Lincoln County published in your issue of the 26th inst. and signed J.H.T., I wish to state that every thing contained therein is false. In reference to Sheriff Brady, I will state that he deposited with our house Territorial funds amounting to nearly $2,000, subject to his order and payable on demand. Owing to sickness in the family of Sheriff Brady he was unable to be in Santa Fe in time to settle his account with the Territory. This I hope will explain satisfactorily how the Gov. in his Message had our County (Lincoln) delinquent. If Mr. J.H.T. was recognized as a gentleman, and could be admitted into respectable circles in our community, he might be better posted in public affairs. For my part, I can't see the object of Mr. J.H.T.'s letter, unless it is to have the public believe that A.A. McSween is one of the largest tax-payers in our County, when in fact he is one of the smallest. Sheriff Brady is ready and willing at any time to show uneasy taxpayers what disposition he has made of the money paid by them; he can also show clean receipts from the Territorial treasurer of his account.
>
> Respectfully,
> J.J. Dolan.[5]

Dolan went after Tunstall's reputation by disarming him with mention of the illness in Brady's family, while simultaneously castigating McSween. A fight appeared imminent through the nasty news columns. With a public airing of sentiment from both sides, Tunstall and Dolan became bitter enemies. On February 6th, at Shedd's ranch, there was an attempt at resolution. However, it went poorly, and both men departed.

After the talks broke down, intimidation followed on the road home. Dolan later reported his version of events to Judge Angel. It stated in part:

> The next morning I went to their camp to see Tunstall about the letter he had written the *Independent*, which was untruthful, and about his attempt to injure us. These facts made me angry; I was armed; I talked to Tunstall in a very severe manner. He acted in a very childish manner. I tried in every way to see if he was a man. He made no resistance although he was armed. I did not drop my carbine on him; I only threw it over my shoulder with the butt towards him.... I told him I was ready to give him any satisfaction he wanted.
>
> Jesse Evans was standing in the corner of the stable near McSween's party's camp. He evidently saw I was excited and followed after me. He did not follow me by request, either directly or indirectly. I had no appointment or engagement with either Baker, Evans or [Jac] Rivers to meet me at San Augustin or anywhere on the road.... The way Evans came to be riding with me in the ambulance from San Augustin was as follows: on account of his being wounded, Evans could not ride in a saddle.... Baker and Rivers followed behind us on horseback. I must confess I was afraid I would be killed on the road, and I did not object to their following after us. At Whitewater, I left Fritz, Longwell, Rivers and Evans, and went on to Tulerosa on horseback, insisting on going alone. But nonwithstanding my request, Baker rode with me as far as Tulerosa. Then he left me, and I went on alone to the Indian Agency, where I obtained conveyance and reached Lincoln.[6]

Dolan explained the details to Angel as if he was arguing self-defense. In fact, he was deposed after the fact. Tunstall's behavior was not mentioned. It was Dolan against Tunstall, not against other ranchers.

According to Dolan, Baker and Evans hardly registered a role in the events leading up to the tragedy.

A series of adversarial meetings between the two sides followed. Frank Baker and several cohorts bunked around the Mescalero Reservation, intimidating associates in the area such as the new U.S. Indian agent, Frederick Godfroy. When McSween's group arrived at the reservation, Baker, Tom Hill, and John Long waited for them. At the least, the constant presence of Evans and Baker constituted harassment. They were not guarding Dolan, and the goal was pure business.[7]

Tunstall and his cowhands reacted. According to Robert Widenmann, a Tunstall and McSween ally, all three and their herdsmen arrived in Lincoln on February 10, 1878 to protest an attachment of property. The next day they recovered a number of horses and mules. McCloskey and Middleton herded them back to the ranch on the Feliz, while Tunstall and the rest of the party followed slowly. On the 13th, Jacob B. "Billy" Mathews, acting on orders as a deputy sheriff of Lincoln County, appeared at the ranch with identified "House" allies George Hindman, John Hurley, Andrew "Buckshot" Roberts, Jessie Evans, and Frank Baker. Mathews talked with Widenmann and explained that any cattle belonging to McSween was subject to seizure. Brewer objected, claiming the cattle on the ranch as his own. The situation was a standoff, but the rancher chanced breaking the tension by inviting the newcomers to dine. According to Widenmann, this achieved nothing. Evans reportedly pointed his rifle towards Widenmann. Baker moved forward and cocked his pistol, expecting trouble. Sensing escalation, Mathews abruptly called off the meeting, then insisted they return to Lincoln for instructions. Baker was notably irritated, and quoted as saying, "What the hell's the use of talking—pitch in and fight and kill the sons of b--s."[8]

The shaded account was obvious, but valuable for the presence of two of the three Blackwater Canyon victims. "Buckshot" Roberts, who later fought these same enemies, was also present. Most importantly, the interaction between Brewer and Baker became personal. For Brewer, the motive of business gave way. The deponent Widenmann, a German-

American with strong political ties to Washington, DC, knew how to answer Angel's diplomatic questions.

Other depositions varied from Widenmann's account of events at the ranch. Mathews stated that his plan was privately discussed with Brewer. Widenmann had no knowledge of it, and he refused any seizure of livestock at their first approach. Brewer and Mathews parleyed alone. After their discussion, all parties declined the offer of breakfast. In another variance from Widenmann's account, John Hurley stated that the German offered breakfast to his adversaries, but they accepted. Regardless of who ate breakfast at Dick Brewer's ranch that morning, Mathews disliked the escalating situation and hardly trusted his own party. In fact, he viewed Evans and Baker as trouble. Sizing up the situation, Mathews left for Lincoln seeking further instructions.[9]

Widenmann's lengthy testimony in the Angel Report traced the actions of William McCloskey. He claimed the old rancher "had been" employed at Tunstall's ranch. He remained in Tunstall's employ on February 13 "as he had been for several weeks previous at rounding up and branding cattle and had made arrangements to work a ranch."[10] Within three days, Widenmann learned that Mathews intended to return. On instructions from Brewer, McCloskey rode with a message to Mathews. He was to warn him that any seizure would result in a lawsuit. Interestingly, the choice of the older man as messenger was twofold, according to Widenmann. He stated, "We sent McCloskey because he was a friend of great number of the party that was reported to be with Matthews [sic]."[11]

McCloskey's mission went awry. According to Widenmann, McCloskey left at three o'clock on the morning of February 18th. He was to deliver the message to Mathews and find a "co-counter" of the cattle taken. McCloskey found Mathews and his posse at the Penasco, and rode with the group in order to complete his instructions. While this occurred, a group comprising Tunstall, Brewer, Middleton, Bonney, Widenmann, and Waite started for town at the break of dawn. Waite drove the wagon while the others rounded up the scattered horses. None of them realized the danger.[12]

Deputy Sheriff Mathews led the large posse, which was broken into two units. While there was no disputing Mathews' leadership, many believed that others—namely Evans, Baker and Hill—were not official posse members. For them, this was personal. They hated Tunstall for taunting them in the Lincoln Jail, so their motive for accompanying the sub-posse was revenge. Mathews was questioned by Angel about the trio, and he answered that they were not deputized. "They were not part of the posse—Evans & Rivers I think met us at the agency—They did not leave with us- but caught up to us about five miles from the agency, this side,—Baker & Hill came to us at the Penasco—They did not meet us at our request either directly or indirectly—We did not know they were there-They said that they were going to the Felix after some horses-"[13]

After he received his orders from Sheriff Brady in Lincoln, Mathews raised a posse of deputized cowhands and rode to the ranch of former Sheriff Hamilton Mills on February 14th. Several days later, they stopped at Paul's Ranch, where Evans and Hill first appeared. The next day, Baker and fellow cowhand Jack Rivers joined up. McCloskey found the group and they all rode north. There was no direct evidence that he relayed the message of peaceful intentions, but given McCloskey's character, it's likely he did as he was told. Mathews was bothered by the presence of Evans and his men. He stated, "they [sic] were around the camp—None of these men were part of the posse—but on the contrary were ordered away by me—We were met here by the party from the Pecos."[14]

Regardless of the composition of the posses, the groups converged at Tunstall's ranch and surrounded the residence. Mathews learned that horses were removed from the property since his previous visit. According to another affidavit from Charles "Dutch Charley" Kreiling, herdsman Henry Brown, who was near the Feliz ranch, informed Mathews' posse that Tunstall and Brewer left for Lincoln. Hearing this, they became alarmed. In Mathews' mind, they were absconding with the livestock. For the sake of speed, it was necessary to form a smaller second group of riders to locate them. Buck Morton led this sub-posse. With two posses searching, Mathews gained wider coverage of the surrounding land. He deputized Morton under the powers of the county, as he felt him qualified to lead this effort.

> I then Deputised [sic] Morton & selected a party to go with him after the horses—and they left. I having instructed them to over take [sic] the horses and bring them back and in case there was any resistance to arrest the men & bring them back to [sic]—If he did not over take them before they reached the plaza (Lincoln) if he found they were going to Lincoln then to follow them in and have Sheriff Brady attach the horses—[15]

The posse split, and the group retrieving the horses sped off. Kreiling confirmed that both Mathews and Dolan warned Morton about Evans and his cohorts. "I heard Mathews tell Morton at the Felix that he did not want Evans, Baker Hill & Davis with the posse. Morton agreed not to let them come, I heard Dolan tell Morton at the Felix just before starting to be very careful and do nothing but what was lawful... Baker Evans, and Hill did not leave with us but followed after the party."[16]

Twenty miles north of the Feliz Ranch, Kreiling noticed Evans and his associates rode alongside the party. Baker's horse was "used up," and he lagged behind the rest of the group. McCloskey accompanied the sub-posse about eight miles north of the ranch, then departed. Six miles further, a report came from the front of the group that several men, possibly Tunstall and Brewer, rode ahead. The lead section of the sub-posse broke off from the trail in fast pursuit. According to Kreiling, this was some 500 yards from the original line of sight.[17]

> When we got up to our party Billy Morton told us that Tunstall was killed—he said he rode up to Tunstall and called on him to surrender holding the papers in his left hand—and that Tunstall pulled his pistol out and fired twice at him, one shot going over his mares neck, and that he Morton then fired & shot Tunstal [sic]—Evans Hill, & Green, came out of the bushes with Morton

after the shooting of Tunstall—Most of our party then went to the place where Tunstall was lying—I found Tunstall lying on his back some blood coming out of his forehead and one foot against or sort of under the saddle, his left foot, the horse was kicking, being wounded in the breast...[18]

According to Kreiling, Tunstall's horse was laid out and shot by an unnamed pursuer. He picked up the Englishman's pistol and noticed two bullets were missing. Four of the party: Kreiling, Hindman, Sam Perry and Wallace Olinger, laid out the body and gathered the horses. All four, as John Hurley and Tom Corcoran, were in the back of the sub-posse.[19]

On the return of the forward party to the remaining body of the sub-posse, the behavior of the assailants changed dramatically. Evans listened, uncharacteristically silent as Morton related the tragic events to the rest of the group. There was a sullen demeanor among the riders. By the time the sub-posse returned to the Felix Ranch, it was about midnight. One of the six or seven horses they gathered died on the way back.[20] When Morton finally reported to Mathews at about 2 a.m., the Virginian told him that he caught up with the horses after thirty miles. Unfortunately, "Tunstall resisted & fired at him & that he returned the fire & Tunstall was killed."[21] As desired, Morton attempted to read out the legal document— informing Tunstall to raise his arms. Instead, Tunstall fired at him. He returned fire and killed the Englishman. Mathews admitted that he lost track of Evans and Baker, but as they claimed some of the stolen horses, they accompanied Morton's group.[22]

Accounts from the other side of the conflict recounted the opposition as more bloodthirsty. Morton stated that his "knife was sharp," and he had a desire to kill someone. During the day, Widenmann reported that Tunstall's party, driving horses, parted with Waite in the wagon. All rode bay horses except Billy the Kid, who rode a gray one. Throughout the day, Tunstall, Brewer and Widenmann remained together, and passed the Pajarito Spring about five o'clock that afternoon. Bonney and Middleton brought up the rear of Tunstall's men—some 500 yards distant.

They crested a ridge and spotted some wild turkeys. Widenmann offered his gun to shoot them, but Tunstall remarked that the German was the better shot and declined to chase the birds. This separated Brewer and Widenmann from Tunstall. They rode 300 yards when they heard men on horseback heading straight for them.[23]

Widenmann shouted a warning to Brewer, and a bullet whizzed between the two men. Without a word, an unknown number of men fired at the pair. The hillside afforded them little cover, so they rode in the open. The group of riders briefly pursued, turned downhill, and moved toward Tunstall. Widenmann and Brewer reached Bonney and Middleton, but they were too late to save the Englishman. However, they did not view the murder, as they had no vantage point from over the ridge. Several gun rapports signaled the violence to them. Four others reached tree cover at the top of the hill and stopped. Therefore, Widenmann and Brewer saw Evans, Baker, Dolan, Pantelion Gallegos, Hindman, Hurley, Hill and Morton.[24]

Morton's sub-posse split between those pursuing the horses and the men they spotted on the ridge. John Hurley was in the middle of the entire group, but when they came across the horses, he stopped to attend to them. However, only vague figures remained visible to him. He later told Frank Angel, "I heard some shots—how many I cannot tell—I was not present when Tunstall was shot-I did not see him shot—nor did I see any one shoot at him—it was scrub timber & a person could not see..."[25] Robert Beckwith, one of Morton's men, gave his version of events. He claimed Tunstall fired at them first, while Morton stopped to read the warrant. Beckwith deposed that "Tunstall commenced to fire at them [Morton, Evans, and Hill] & fired two shots one just passing over the neck of Mortons horse that thereupon they (Evans Hill & Morton) fired at Tunstall & Tunstall was shot-"[26]

Conclusions could be drawn from the varying depositions. It was possible that Beckwith confirmed Morton's version, but it also corroborated Widenmann's testimony of Tunstall's bad aim with a gun. In either case, Tunstall's death was not personal to Morton. From the collective details gathered in the reports, a few conclusions approached concensus. These are:

- Morton carried the warrant.
- Morton shot Tunstall or took the credit for the shooting.
- Evans and Hill were present during Tunstall's death.
- Baker may have been present at the murder site, depending on the condition of his horse.
- Tunstall's horse was shot and killed by one of them.

British authorities made official inquiries, and Washington responded by sending Frank Angel to sort out the details. His official account contained cross-complaints and denials from witnesses on both sides. The accuracy of his deponents fell victim in this process, and Angel never solved the crime. The numerous depositions contained many details, but more finger-pointing. The category of accounts neatly divided between those nearest the site of the murder, usually siding with the Dolan-Murphy faction, or Tunstall's allies. Most of the Englishman's friends and employees lived far away, so they had a disadvantage in relating their accounts to Angel. The result was a "whodunit" with a complex series of errors.

Given the shaded accounts in the report, Angel suspected several people of Tunstall's murder. He wrote in his summary, "Who shot Tunstall will never be Known [sic] But [sic] there is no doubt that Wm. S. Morton, Jesse Evans and Hill were the only persons present and saw the shooting, and that two of these persons murdered him."[27] Angel's conclusions followed the official inquest on Tunstall, which began on February 19th. Justice of the Peace John Wilson gathered a jury of six citizens: George P. Barber, R.W. Gilbert, Benjamin Ellis, John Newcomb, Samuel Smith, and Frank B. Coe. The conclusion was hasty and vague. They found that Tunstall died "by means of divers[sic] bullets shot and sent forth out of and from deadly weapons there and then held by one or more of the men who names are herewith written: Jessie Evans, Frank Baker, Thos. Hill, G. Hindman, J.J. Dolan, William Morton and others not identified..."[28]

One interesting and overlooked theory revolved around Morton's admission of shooting Tunstall. Evans, Hill and Baker were not officially part of the posse, and if his superior Mathews learned they were present, Morton feared trouble given the previous warnings. In his mind, the death of Tunstall read better as a botched capture than a dishonorable murder. Obviously, the people with the best knowledge kept quiet.

On March 2, 1878, the inquest was certified by Justice of the Peace Wilson and the jurors. In response to the findings, Dolan denied his presence at the site of the murder. As there was no other notable documentation to compare to the results of the inquest, the depositions stand on their own. Like the aftermath of several violent episodes in the West, the inquest stirred public outrage. In this case, the results failed to mollify either side. Shortly afterward, a group of Tunstall allies drew their own conclusions and decided on their next course of action.[29]

The inquest proved the turning point to the real roots of the Lincoln County War. There were two elements present after the Tunstall murder that were not there previously. The leadership of the "House," Chisum and the independent ranchers lost control of the situation completely. The new contenders for power were the cowhands, not the ranch leadership. In fact, the powerful ranchers and merchants became side characters after the death of Tunstall. Dolan proved the only leadership figure who maintained some control. The other element was a change of motive. Business was no longer a goal.

The Tunstall murder went unsolved by the inquest and the conflicting affidavits in the Angel Report. As these comprised the instrumental documents surrounding the death of Tunstall, historians sorted through the material again in the 1950s. Rasch asked correspondent and researcher Paul Sann about his evidence that Morton and Evans did the killing, as relayed by Alexander McSween's testimony to Angel, but as before, the answer was inconclusive. Finally, Lincoln County War enthusiast Steve Sederwall investigated the Tunstall murder site in April of 2005. With a team of researchers, Sederwall combed the area and traced the trajectory of the chase using law enforcement tactics. He ascertained the direction and natural landmarks, such as the generational nests of wild turkeys that the Regulators chased for dinner that evening. The feathers of their descendants littered the ground. Using the resources available, he found the casing of a lone bullet—the one that killed Tunstall. He compared the trajectory of the bullet to the depositions in the Angel Report, and while there was still no identity to the assassin, the common elements of the accounts proved factual.[30]

5

THE CAPTURE AND TRAIL TO BLACKWATER

Once the outline of the Lincoln County War was defined, the actions grew more personal to the cowhands. Beginning after the death of John Henry Tunstall, his allies retaliated. Both federal and local authorities searched for Jessie Evans in Lincoln, and Justice of the Peace Wilson issued warrants against the members of Morton's sub-posse. Miguel Otero, in his account *The Real Billy the Kid*, related that Sheriff Brady appeared disinterested in the search for the killers of Tunstall, so McSween turned to Wilson, "an eccentric old codger, who for a few drinks of whisky would sign almost anything."[1]

It was hardly a ringing endorsement for Wilson, but McSween pressed for the advantage. In the May 4, 1878 issue of the *Santa Fe New Mexican,* he recounted the events that preceded the search for the alleged assassins. "Warrants were then sworn out before Squire Wilson against the persons who composed the posse of the deputy—sheriff Matthews [sic] when Tunstall was killed. Then warrants were placed in R.M. Brewer's hands and he took a posse of twelve men and went after Morton, Baker and others. He arrested these two men and started for Lincoln..."[2]

McSween's account was overly simplistic. The names on the three issued warrants were Morton, Baker, and a cowhand named Tom Cochran, who was implicated for stealing Tunstall cattle and the murder of several teenagers. Cochran, sometimes spelled Cochlan or Coghlan in records, later escaped to Arizona. Brewer located Morton and Baker at a place known as Howell's Arroyo, halfway between the bed of Seven Rivers and the Penasco. It was owned by "Cap" Amazon Howell, an ally of Jimmy Dolan. The pair, on horseback, fled at the sight of Brewer's men.

After chasing them several miles, the horses carrying Morton and Baker gave out, and they fled on foot.[3]

In March 1928, an article by Roswell resident Jim Miller revealed details of Morton and Baker's capture. On March 6, 1878, Brewer, Bonney and nine others surprised Morton, Baker, and a third man, Sam Lloyd, near the Penasco River. The posse ignored Lloyd and chased the other pair as they fled. After six miles, the horses Morton and Baker rode broke down. They dismounted and ran into a thicket of tule. The Regulators lit the thickets afire, and the air filled with arid smoke. Morton's legs emitted a cold sweat as he pondered a way out. After they secured acceptable terms for surrender and a safe conduct promise from Brewer, the men came out with their hands up. According to Miller, Morton related this version of events several days after his capture, when at the Chisum ranch.[4]

Several historians disagreed with Miller's account of the capture. In June 1957, researcher and collector Al Erwin wrote Phil Rasch that Mrs. Viola Slaughter, daughter of Cap Howell, related that "...a Posse [sic] came looking for three fellows, Billy Morton, Frank Baker, and Tom Cochran, they tried to get them to disguise in womens clothes with Bonnetts [sic], and hike down the arroya... Tom hid in the corn crib, Morton, Baker were captured."[5] Mullin's notes disputed unconditional surrender. Only the threat of fire existed. It was also doubtful Morton and Baker wore women's clothing to disguise themselves. To support Mullin's analysis, this news would spread far and wide. Erwin, who later wrote a biography on Slaughter, suggested that it was Cochran who was offered woman's clothing, but he refused.[6]

In his description of the capture, Frazier Hunt's 1956 book, The Tragic Days of Billy the Kid, was sketchy in certain areas. However, the book held together in large part to Fulton's input to the research. "It was around noon on the second day when they flushed a human covey of five in the rough country below the lower Penasco. The men were resting in the shade of a lone tree, the split reins of their bridles dangling on the ground, when the Brewer posse suddenly appeared over a rise a hundred yards or so away. In a matter of seconds the wanted men grabbed up their loose reins and vaulted into their saddles."[7] Hunt's book contained details on the capture that are not presented elsewhere. Further on, Morton and Baker broke from a group of five horsemen, and Brewer allowed the other three to escape. The other three were allegedly Cochran, Lloyd, and an unknown cowhand. This made sense as Morton supervised the cow camp, but slightly varied from the Miller account of the capture. However, there was enough common agreement in both versions.[8]

> Some of the horses in the posse were beginning to play out, but Brewer and the Kid and two or three others were closing in when the pair wheeled their ponies sharply to the right. For a few seconds their mounts presented a broadside, and there was more shooting. Stumbling and spent the two horses went down at almost the same moment.
> The two men found their feet and by luck reached a sort of sink hole in the center of a basin once overgrown with tall cattails. It gave them temporary protection. Apparently one of the pair had pulled out his Winchester before his horse fell, and he was able now to hold back the men on horseback.
> The siege was a dreary one. Finally, beaten down by thirst and hunger and with ammunition almost gone, the two men accepted Brewer's promise of protection.[9]

Hunt's version curiously omitted any mention of fire or smoke. However, the basic facts were all present: the horses tired, the two hid amongst cattails and later surrendered. Given both Hunt and Miller generally agreed, this was the likely scenario. Miller's devices of fiery tule thickets and resulting sweat were probably literary flourishes.

Other sources emphasized Brewer's offer of conditional surrender, and the Kid's renunciation of it to Morton and Baker. A ranch hand named Pink Simms wrote Fulton in May 1932 that he believed it was a conditional surrender. According to Simms, Billy the Kid was unhappy about a safe conduct, though he was not present during the capture. The Kid followed his own code, and thereby broke the rules that Brewer intended to follow.[10]

> The Kid was not present when (Morton and Baker) were captured after being promised safe conduct by Brewer. The Kid was furnious [sic] when he found out the posse had promised them that they would not be killed. It was suggested that they be murdered anyway. Billito quickly vetoed that, stating that it was impossible after they had given their word not to do so...unless they 'made a break...'[11]

The Authentic History of Billy the Kid, partially ghostwritten by Upson, but credited to Pat Garrett, gave the same version of the capture under a negotiated safe conduct with Brewer. This version included literary license, such as the line—"The Kid's Winchester belched fire continually, and his followers were not idle..."[12] As the Kid's presence was questionable, this bit of bravado was followed by an unrealistic sequence. The horses suddenly fell at the same moment, to which Morton and Baker fled to a sinkhole. They, according to Garrett's book, "could have stood off twice the force," but felt the wisdom of surrender under a safe conduct rather than starve. Billy the Kid objected to the safe conduct, but was restrained from his initial impulses. *Authentic Life* stated the Kid rode in the advance party after the capture, muttering to himself, "My time will come."[13]

Burn's version in *The Saga of Billy the Kid* not only included Bonney in the capturing party, but incorrectly promoted him to leadership during the capture. He stated that they fought for two days and nights at the Howell dugout, and that a parley secured them terms of surrender. The conversational portion, which Morton called out, "We'll surrender ... if you'll give us your word we won't be killed," sounded like a campfire story. Both Morton and Baker extended a greeting to the Kid, who coldly rebuffed them with "I don't know you and don't want to know you."[14]

South Spring Ranch

In hindsight, the Kid intended to cross the line in disobeying Brewer's intent. This became apparent after the capture—and ensured that the powers within the New Mexico Territory no longer controlled events. Brewer learned this lesson the hard way.

One of the best primary sources for this time period was the diary kept by Sallie Chisum. According to her great-granddaughter and namesake, Sallie Chisum Robert, there was no intimate relationship between her ancestor and Billy the Kid. Despite his gift of two cameo hearts on August 22, 1878, this was between friends. Members of the Maxwell family sent Sallie pictures, while another friend, Charles Pierce, sent her a ring and pin. Regardless, Sallie was unmarried. Her father James supervised the South Spring Ranch. At various times, he or his brother John employed many of these same men as workers in the business. To the Chisums, Billy the Kid was just another cowboy. South Spring was both a place of employment and a sanctuary to herdsmen.[15]

In December 1874, John Chisum traded 2,400 head of cattle for the forty acres comprising South Spring Ranch. It was an inspired location near an artesian well and the confluence of two rivers. The Chisums built an eight-room house, complete with corral and patio as the centerpiece of the property. The "Square House" figured prominently as Chisum's headquarters in the spring of 1875. The operation continued, even during a period that John was captured in March 1878. James ran operations when the cattle king was "detained" in the town of Las Vegas.[16]

Sallie's diary detailed the night Morton and Baker arrived. Burns interpreted portions of these memories, albeit erroneously, in *Saga of Billy the Kid*, which later resurfaced in Coe's *Frontier Fighter*.[17] The text of the latter book condensed the actions without any conversational flourishes.

'They put the prisoners in my room for the night because it was the only room in the house that did not have an outside exposure. None of us slept. We did not discuss it, but we knew that the boys were doomed. A guard, armed to the teeth, watched them to prevent any possibility of escape. They were nice looking young chaps with unmistakable marks of culture. The next morning young Baker gave me a bunch of keepsakes including a pretty gold watch, and requested me to send them to his sweetheart, Miss Lizzie Lester, in Syracuse, New York if anything happened to him.'[18]

Sallie Chisum's sympathy for the captured cowboys was evident in her sorrowful description of Buck Morton's departure. "When Morton bade me good-bye, he could not speak. He simply gripped my hand. He was from a good family of Virginia. These fellows came here to make good, but fell into the easy-going road to ruin."[19]

Sallie Chisum's brother Will drew a hand-drawn floor plan of the South Spring Ranch. It revealed three bedrooms in the main house, and two interior entrances. The bedroom used for detaining Morton and Baker opened internally between an office on one side and another interior room, making escape impossible for the pair. The only other bedroom that merited consideration as a holding cell was a smaller corner space— which boasted a fireplace.[20]

In Roswell, the most prominent witness of the activities of the prisoners was Ash Upson, the town's "jack-of-all-trades." An educated Connecticut native, Upson tried several occupations as he approached the age of fifty. It was over a decade before wanderlust brought him to the New Mexico Territory. Using his writing skills, Upson established himself in the newspaper trade. In July 1870, the *Santa Fe New Mexican* read, "Ash Upson left yesterday for Las Vegas to establish a newspaper."[21]

The following year Upson purchased a newspaper, the *Elizabethtown Telegraph*, and relocated the presses a short journey south to Las Vegas. The result was *The Mail*, published by Upson and a partner named Bolinger. However, this arrangement only lasted a year. Upson left the venture and headed south once again. He appeared in the town of Lincoln, newly re-named from its Spanish name—La Placita. During a few days stay, Upson met Texan Robert Casey, who owned a ranch near the settlement of Picacho, about twenty miles east of Lincoln. He stayed at the Casey Ranch as a teacher, and met John Chisum. When the cattle king needed a surveyor for his new lands at South Spring Ranch, Upson took the job. He always intended to return to the Casey Ranch, but a request kept him at the budding village—soon to be known as Roswell.[22]

>   This place Roswell, is four miles from Chisum's principle ranch and there is no one living here except F.G. Christy, the acting postmaster. He is an old California miner, and is very dissatisfied here all alone, and making nothing except a small salary for looking out for the property. I did not wish to return to Mrs. Casey's until I had completed my survey, and Mr. Christie ugently [sic] requested me to remain with him, and to promise to accept the postmasters [sic] position with the prerequisites etc. I consented to stay for the present.[23]

In the 1920s, Maurice Fulton sought out Upson's family, and found his niece, Florence Downs Muzzy, in New York. She spent time in New Mexico, and while conversing with Fulton, mentioned Sallie Chisum Robert and her connection to the capture of Morton and Baker. In a letter to Fulton, Muzzy wrote that Sallie's bedroom held both captives. "She [Sallie Robert] knew Uncle Ash, and knew Billy the Kid—and told me about her father's store in Roswell, & how Billy & his gang spent the night there, obeying her injunction to wash up the dishes before they left in the morning! She said she had a barred window to her sleeping room."[24]

On the morning of March 9, 1878, Ash Upson worked in the Roswell post office as the party approached. Although western novelist Emerson Hough barely mentioned the event in *Story of the Outlaw*, primarily based on interviews with Garrett, he wrote, "Baker and Morton surrendered under promise of safekeeping, and were held for a time at Roswell."[25] Upson's version of events during this episode in *Authentic Life* gained more credibility, mostly due to his first-hand account.

...They stopped at Roswell, five miles from Chisum's, to give Morton an opportunity to mail a letter at the postoffice [sic] there. This letter he registered to a cousin, Hon. H.H. Marshall, Richmond, Va. A copy of this letter is in the hands of the author, as well as a letter subsequently addressed to the postmaster by Marshall. Morton was descended from the best blood of Virginia, and left many relatives and friends to mourn his loss. Morton, together with all the rest of the party, was well known to the postmaster, M.A. Upson, and Morton requested him, should any important event transpire, to write to his cousin and inform him of the facts connected therewith. Upson asked him if he apprehended danger to himself on the trip. He replied that he did not, as the posse had pledged themselves to deliver him and Baker to the authorities at Lincoln. But he added that, in case this pledge was violated, he wished his people to be informed. McCloskey of the Brewer posse was standing by, and rejoined, speaking to Morton, "Billy, if harm comes to you two they will have to kill me first."[26]

Through the Garrett book, Upson wrote that Billy the Kid appeared "distrait and sullen" at the post office, and they stayed only a short time before moving towards Lincoln—at ten in the morning. Six hours later, Martin Chaves of Picacho arrived at the post office and stated that the posse and prisoners ventured off the main road towards Aqua Negra.[27]

Miguel Otero's *Real Billy the Kid* included more insight into Bonney's behavior at this time. Written in the 1930s, Otero wrote in greater detail than what seemed plausible. He included exact quotations in conversation between the subjects, which could be attributed to Upson himself. The conversation went as follows: "Upson asked: "Do you expect anything to happen to you?" "I don't," said Morton. "The posse has pledged itself to deliver us safely to the authorities at Lincoln, but in case the pledge is violated I want my people to be informed."[28]

One interesting detail gleaned from Jim Miller's 1928 articles in the *Roswell Daily Record* was that Upson's relationship with the Chisums soured. His alliance with two other local residents, Heiskell Jones and Marion Turner, turned their sympathies toward Dolan and Murphy. According to Miller, Upson served as a U.S. Land Commissioner, unattainable without the support of the "House" leadership. Miller's brother Will formed an alliance with James Chisum and another business partner, Bob Gilbert. The object was purely business, as "the first ditch taking water out of South-spring River on the north side."[29]

The shifting set of alliances created competing accounts. Will Miller, allied to the Chisums, told the story of the capture of Morton and Baker to his brother. He wrote that Upson's version was wrong. Despite meandering narrative, he related the actions in rich detail.

> The Tooley in which they were hiding was on fire, the surrender was unconditional and of course they expected to be young hero [sic] of the War over at Chisum's. I went over to Chisum's house and there I met [MacNab] and The Kid. He had met my brother often. He was sitting on the counter of Chisum's commissary. He was telling of the Bottomless Lakes…It was true McLoskey [sic] had promised Morten [sic] and Baker safe delivery if it was in his power to do so, but that was after they arrived at the Chisum Ranch and that was said in a low tone that he did not intend the Kid or MacNabb [sic] to hear; but they knew that was why he volunteered his services and that he was acting in disguise, and was really a friend of Baker and Morten [sic].[30]

In his article, Miller disagreed with Upson about the capture of Morton and Baker. His brother had first-hand knowledge of the event, and Miller himself wrote a friend in Texas that "Ash Upson's story about having been as one [of] the family of Billy's mother is all bunk. I do not believe that upson [sic] ever met Billy until after Tunstall's murderers were killed in Black Water Canyon, because I heard Upson make a sarcastic remark in regard to that strip of a boy they called the Kid's acts during the war."[31]

Perhaps silence was the best judge of who was right. A clipping of the Miller's 1928 interview was found in Sallie Chisum Robert's papers, both unmarked and unquestioned. As she marked other papers, her absence of comment decided the correct version. Sallie's nature caught any erring detail, and this was one of a few clippings she kept on the Lincoln County War. There were plenty more articles on Thomas Edison.[32]

Sallie Chisum Robert and family, at a picnic near Artesia, New Mexico. Courtesy of Sallie Chisum Robert, great-granddaughter of subject.

Morton and Baker received some allowances in Roswell. The penning and delivery of Morton's famous final letter was the prime example. The letter was posted to his cousin Judge Marshall in Virginia. Its damning accusations provided a blueprint for the murders. However, the plot to kill them originated *after* the letter was posted, and perhaps on the road to Lincoln itself. Another possibility was that the moderates in the capturing party, namely Brewer, Middleton, or McCloskey, allowed the delivery without the knowledge of the others. Either way, Dick Brewer controlled the outcome in Roswell.[33]

The famous letter was a stinging indictment as much as a goodbye to his relatives. Morton was no fool, and clearly suspected foul play.

South Spring River, N.M.
March 8, 1878

H.H. Marshall
Richmond, Va.

Dear Sir:

Some time since I was called upon to assist in serving a writ of attachment on some property wherein resistance had been made against the law.

The parties had started off with some horses which should be attached, and I as deputy sheriff with a posse of twelve men was sent in pursuit of same. We overtook them, and while attempting to serve the writ our party was fired on by one J.H. Tunstall, the balance of the party having ran off. The fire was returned and Tunstall was killed. This happened on the 18th of February.

The 6th of March I was arrested by a constable's party, accused of the murder of Tunstall. Nearly all of the sheriff's party fired at him, and it is impossible for any one to say who killed him. When the party which came to arrest me, and one man who was with me, first saw us about one hundred yards distant, we started in another direction when they (eleven in number) fired nearly one hundred shots at us. We ran about five miles, when both of our horses fell and we made a stand. When they came up, they told us if we would give up, they would not harm us.

After talking awhile, we gave up our arms and were made prisoners. There was one man in the party who wanted to kill me after I had surrendered, and was restrained with the greatest difficulty by others of the party. The constable himself said he was sorry we gave up as he had not wished to take us alive. We arrived here last night enroute to Lincoln. I have heard that we were not to be taken alive to that place. I am not at all afraid of their [sic] killing me, but if they should do so, I wish that the matter should be investigated and the parties dealt with according to law. If you do not hear from me in four days after receipt of this, I would like you to make inquiries about the affair.

The names of the parties who have arrested me are: R.M. Brewer, J.G. Skurlock [sic], Chas. Bowdre, Wm. Bonney, Henry Brown, Frank McNab, "Wayt," Sam Smith, Jim French (and two others named McCloskey and Middleton who are friends). There are two parties in arms, and violence is expected. The military are at the scene of disorder and trying to keep peace. I will arrive at Lincoln the night of the 10th and will write you immediately if I get through safe. Have been in the employ of Jas. J. Dolan & Co. of Lincoln for eighteen months since the 9th of March '77 and have been getting $60.00 per month. Have about six hundred dollars due me from them and some horses, etc., at their cattle camps.

I hope if it becomes necessary that you will look into this affair, if anything should happen, I refer you to T.B. Catron, U.S. Attorney of Santa Fe, N.M. and Col. Rynerson, District Attorney, La Mesilla, N.M. They both know all about the affair as the writ of attachment was issued by Judge Warren Bristol, La Mesilla, N.M. and everything was legal. If I am taken safely to Lincoln, I will have no trouble, but will let you know.

If it should be as I suspect, please communciate [sic] with my brother, Quin Morton, Lewisburg, W. Va. Hoping that you will attend to this affair if it becomes necessary and excuse me for troubling you if does not,

> I remain
> Yours respectfully,
> W.S. Morton[34]

Lincoln,
   Lincoln Co. N.M.

Although unknown how Judge Marshall reacted to the letter, there must have been shock and concern. A search of Marshall's papers revealed no reaction or mention of a return letter to Upson. Given the business-like writing of a jurist, his emotions remained hidden in many of his writings.[35]

A rare insight into the character of Judge Marshall was offered by his grandson, Henry Venable Gaines. He wrote of a serious and "small man—probably 5 feet 7 or 8 inches Tall—on the thin side. He had bright black eyes & gray hair (what there was of it); impatient with the stupidity of people in general & Especially [sic] with the stupidity of servants & children..."[36]

The posting of Morton's letter was a cooperative effort between its author, Upson and at least one captor. Given the wording presented in the letter itself, the delivery person was one of the "friends" mentioned—McCloskey or Middleton. Upson gladly posted it, as his anger at Chisum gave him an incentive to make trouble.

Once the group reached Roswell, word was sent to Dolan's allies in Lincoln. The leader of the Seven Rivers Warriors, Milo Pierce, told Jim Miller his own account of these events in 1918. Miller in turn wrote, "... when they heard that The Kid and party had these men Morten [sic] and Baker holding them at the Chisum Ranch, that all of those who called themselves the Seven Rivers Warriors, together with all the Dolen [sic] and Murphy crew—which Pierce said numbered about 70 men—started from Lincoln for the Chisum Ranch, to take the prisoners and their guard to the Lincoln Court House; but The Kid and party was just a little too early for them." This was a logical reaction, as there was reason for concern. Given Sheriff Brady's loyalties to the "House," Brewer expected trouble should he turn his prisoners into his custody.[37]

The fight started up in the newspapers as well. Those organs controlled by the opposing factions varied their slant on the events of March 9th. A letter to the editor in the *Mesilla Independent* on April 21st, stated,

Warrants were sworn out before J.B. WILSON (who was acting as justice of the Peace by appointment of the county commissioners) for the arrest of all concerned in the killing of Tunstall: these warrants were placed in the hands of RICHARD BRUER [sic], who was specially appointed as constable to serve them. Bruer [sic], accompanied by a *posse* of eleven men arrested BAKER and MORTON, who, together with one of the *posse* named McClosky [sic], were killed: there is no doubt that they were deliberately killed, after they had surrendered. BAKER was one of the EVANS gang of outlaws: MORTON is said to have been a different kind of man: both of them however were present at and participated in Tunstall's murder.[38]

The posse marched north from Roswell. After a day's ride, the group stopped in "friendly" territory. Somewhere between Roswell and Blackwater Canyon, the mumbling began. The two prisoners, and possibly McCloskey, needed to die. A road, primarily used by the Spanish sheepherders, forked north of Picacho. They took their prisoners down the sharp trail toward Los Palos Springs, who according to historian Clarence Siringo Adams, was settled by three Spanish-speaking families who relocated there from Colorado. The families felt a kinship to the Regulators, and in particular William Bonney. One old time resident, Mrs. J.A. Manning, recalled the Kid's visit to her home. With her brother, Charlie Ballard, she recounted Indian stories and concluded that "he was a likeable person."[39]

Likeable or not, the truth was that three men lay dead in Blackwater Canyon. There was no question that it was friendly territory for the Regulators. The suspects tried to justify their confusing actions, but the echoes of the gun resounded in print and law. As the plans for the shooting was <u>after</u> Roswell, the Lincoln County War truly began with their deaths. The Kid started it, but a question remained. How much of the Kid's actions were based on the death of Tunstall or hatred for rivals Morton and Baker? Regardless of the answer to this question, a war of words and deeds ensued, and most of Brewer's posse died shortly and violently afterward.

6

DAMNATION OF THE REGULATORS

Thirty-three year-old Frank Angel was a practicing attorney when assigned the investigation of the murder of John Tunstall and related events in New Mexico Territory. In April 1878, both the Justice and State Departments felt the pressure of the escalating violence. Angel conducted several interlocking investigations, including a serious inquiry into the practices of Territorial Governor Samuel Axtell. The Governor faced mounting criticism over the "Santa Fe Ring." His reputation suffered mightily, but the death of British subject Tunstall forced open an investigation. Once he reached Santa Fe, Angel lost no time in gathering information. After a few days conversing with Territorial officials, Angel visited pertinent witnesses in Lincoln. The meticulous lawyer kept a comment-filled notebook on all the characters he met, as chronicled by historian Lee Scott Theisen. For example, Jessie Evans was castigated by Angel as a "Lincoln Co—outlaw—murderer-."[1]

As Frank Angel gathered facts, renewed violence broke out in Lincoln County. Wholesale war was imminent after the executions of Morton, Baker, and McCloskey. Their deaths brought retaliatory actions from the gunslingers on each side. The "House" and the independent ranchers were shuffled to the side as the cowboys took matters into their own hands. A series of ambushes and counterstrikes afflicted their ranks. Of those guarding Morton and Baker in Blackwater Canyon as their prisoners, MacNab and Brewer, the two leaders, both died shortly afterward. Lincoln County Sheriff William Brady and his deputy, George Hindman, planned the persecution of Brewer's posse, but died in an ambush as they rode through Lincoln on April 1.

The Regulators struck back with varied results. Three days later, at Blazer's Mill, Brewer met his maker at the hands of Andrew "Buckshot" Roberts, who also died in the gunfight. MacNab was ambushed a short distance from Blackwater Canyon. Even after the Lincoln County War concluded, the Regulators from Blackwater Canyon lost more among their ranks. Bowdre fell in the famous gunfight at Stinking Springs in December 1880 that preceded the capture of the Kid. Waite, Middleton, and Brown left the area and escaped the pattern—though their fates varied.[2]

Jessie Evans also avoided the fate of Morton and Baker. He was not present in Blackwater Canyon the day his former allies died, for he and compatriot Tom Hill botched a robbery near Tularosa. While considered safe territory for Evans in the past, the pair met stiff resistance from their intended victim, an armed peddler. Hill was killed and Evans badly wounded. Shortly after, he limped into Fort Stanton and surrendered rather than chance death. After a time behind bars and subsequent unpleasant episodes in Lincoln, he resumed his criminal career in Texas. Then he was again captured, this time by the Texas Rangers. Imprisoned at Huntsville and sentenced to hard labor, Evans managed to escape again and completely vanished in 1882.[3]

The leadership of the Regulators was itself a curse. Although some texts incorrectly noted his leadership, the Kid wisely avoided it. During the period of the Blackwater murders, Dick Brewer was well respected, and John Chisum and 163 others signed a memorial that Angel kept in his official papers. They lamented the death of "a young man of irreproachable character, who commanded the respect and admiration of all who knew him.... He was a hard working, generous, sober, upright and noble minded young man."[4]

After Blazer's Mill and the demise of Brewer, Frank MacNab picked up the mantle of leadership of the Regulators. According to correspondence between Mullin and Rasch, MacNab's experience ranked highly within the Chisum organization. Mullin called him at one point in his career, "Chisum's right hand man." A natural fit, MacNab followed

Brewer in succession as leader of the Regulators. However, his term was a short one. On April 30, 1878, with the Coes and a cowhand named Ab Saunders, he paid for his role in the Blackwater Canyon killings. They rode down the Hondo Valley and straight into a trap.[5]

A writer who called himself "Outsider" wrote an account of MacNab's death in the *Mesilla Independent*. "Outsider" was probably Upson, who kept up with any event near Roswell. With a byline that remarked "Frank McNab killed!" the details were reported to all readers.

Editors INDEPENDENT;

> On the evening of the 29th ult., Frank McNab, James A. Saunders and Frank Coe of the "Regulator" party left the town of Lincoln for Coe & Saunders ranche [sic] 4 miles below Joseph Storm's place. When they approached Chas. Fritz's place Coe, who was riding about 100 yards ahead of McNab and Saunders saw some 20 horses standing about the place, all three of the men had their guns in their scabbards, not expecting what so soon followed: as they approached the house their [sic] were fired upon by a party of men concealed in Fritz's house, garden and blacksmith shop. The volley killed the horses ridden by the three men, and they were deprived of all means of escape. The firing was continued until Frank McNab was killed, and Saunders severely wounded in the left foot and hip. Frank Coe was taken prisoner, the attacking party stating that they intended to keep him as a hostage. It should be stated that Mr. Charles Fritz was not at home at the time and the women were powerless to prevent the party from taking possession [sic] of the house.[6]

MacNab and Saunders lay dead, and Frank Coe was imprisoned in the Dolan store in Lincoln. The next day, most of the assigned guards left the location to attend to the gunfire at the McSween House and Tunstall store. The remaining guard, Wallace Olinger, released him. Coe ran to the nearby Ellis House, where fighting flared up hours later. The arrival of the Ninth U.S. Cavalry defused the gunplay, arrested most of the troublemakers, and prevented expansion of the conflict. However, it was inevitable—the Seven Rivers cowboys became hunted.[7]

MacNab's death may have been premeditated. In 1937, resident Francisco Trujillo gave his account of the ambush to Works Progress Administration worker Edith Crawford. He claimed Baker was a relative of Robert Baker, the owner of a ranch near Seven Rivers. Lincoln County Constable Anastasio Martinez responded to family inquiries and formed a posse for the hunt. According to Trujillo, it was on Robert Baker's order that MacNab was killed.

> When [Constable] Anastasio Martinez, John Scroggin and Billy the Kid and I arrived at the door of the cabin, Juan Armijo spoke up and said, 'How are you, Kiko?' 'Come on out' I said to Juan. When he came out I asked him 'Did you kill McNabb?' He said 'Yes, I killed him on Robert Baker's order. He said that I didn't kill him he [Baker] would kill me. So I then went out to where McNabb [sic] was hiding behind some trees, using them as a shield against those who were firing at him from the house, and killed him.'[8]

Armijo died almost immediately. Assailants named in the MacNab ambush were Morton's allies-the Beckwiths and Olingers, and Dick Lloyd, who escaped the fate of his friends. News accounts of the time also mentioned Charles Martin, Lewis Paxton, Joe Nash, John Long, Sam and Thomas Cochran, Tom Green, Sam Perry, Jim Ramer, "Dutch Charlie" Kruling, John Galvin, and Milo Pierce. In the *Cimarron News and Press*, "Soapweed"—probably Widenmann—wrote sarcastically that the men "claim to be acting under orders from the late Sheriff Brady. Peppin and Mathews claim that, as his deputies, they have warrants for Brewer and party for arresting the late Morton and Baker!!"[9]

Equally unlikely was the news account from the opposite side. "El Gato" wrote a week later in the *New Mexican* that MacNab was "riddled with bullets," and that Coe and Saunders "begged like dogs" as "having in view the actions of their party" after the fate of Morton and Baker. No other recounting—including Trujillo's account—mentioned the captives begging for their lives. Neither Coe nor Saunders were present during the capture and death of Morton and Baker, but apparently "El Gato" did not discriminate.[10]

With the death of MacNab, leadership of the Regulators fell to Scurlock, yet another member of the team that killed Morton and Baker. Known as "Doc" because of his early medical training in New Orleans, Scurlock held a position as deputy under the new county sheriff, John Copeland, in the late spring of 1878. Unlike Sheriff Brady, Copeland proved a sympathetic ally to the McSween interests. Although a competent official, Copeland was ousted in favor of Vermont native and former soldier George "Dad" Peppin. Only after the death of McSween in July 1878 did William Bonney assume a quasi-leadership role in the Regulators.[11]

The Kid achieved his leading position through attrition among his allies. While the actions of Bowdre and Doc Scurlock received emphasis in the late spring of 1878, many knew the latter was the real leader. Phil Rasch felt the Kid's youth prevented his immediate succession in the Regulator ranks, but was "greatly disappointed that there is so little on [Jessie] Evans. Also, I am a little surprised that my friend Henry Brown seems to be almost unmentioned. I had thought that he was more prominent [than] he seems to have been."[12]

Henry Newton Brown was destined for a delayed, but violent, death. He was one of the few Regulators who inspired newsprint after the Lincoln County War. Like some of the other Regulators, Brown left the New Mexico Territory in pursuit of a career change in Texas, and later in Kansas. After the round of violence that culminated in McSween's death, the heat on the Regulators intensified. A number of them drifted north towards Las Vegas, then east to the panhandle town of Tascosa, Texas. In October, Brown quit the gang and became a local lawman. For a year, he tracked horse thieves as deputy sheriff for Oldham County, Texas, and then became a constable in Tascosa. While most of the Regulators drifted back to New Mexico Territory, Brown mended his own fences. After a short stint as constable, he resumed work on the cattle trails and made his way to Caldwell, Kansas.[13]

In Kansas, Brown sowed the seeds of his own demise. By 1883, Henry Brown was a reformed criminal chasing his former kind. He found work as a lawman in Caldwell, but shocked citizens there in April 1884, when Brown, Deputy Ben Wheeler, and two others attempted a bank robbery. Two bank employees died, and the suspects were captured. Although taken to jail, a mob determined to hang the robbers. In one of history's strangest ironies, Brown wrote his wife a final letter on April 30, 1884, which was reminiscent of Buck Morton's last message to his cousin. Like Morton, Brown suspected a group of people might kill him. His prediction proved correct, as the mob succeeded in hanging his three associates and shot him making a break for freedom.[14]

Although not as similar a fate as their former victims in Blackwater Canyon, others in the Brewer posse suffered stranger fates. One of these was John Middleton. Although reportedly a moderate in the group, he left the area shortly after his interview with Frank Angel. However, his nerve proved immoderate in his later actions. After drifting to Kansas, he sent a series of ill-advised letters to Tunstall's father. He married and operated a store for a time, but proved too restless for a sedate lifestyle. Several versions circulated over his fate, including one found by Rasch. After moving to Bastrop, Texas for a time, he returned to New Mexico Territory. Upon his return he contracted a disease and died. A second, and more grandiose, version was that Middleton grew restless in Kansas, and worked his way to the Indian Territory in 1882. There he met the famous female bandit Belle Starr, became her lover, and started anew. This version was extolled through Edwin P. Hicks' 1963 book, *Belle Starr and Her Pearl*. The book had an interesting plot twist on Middleton. Belle had Middleton shot, and her own death in 1889 was an act of vengeance carried out by his brother.[15]

Historians traced Middleton's movements to ascertain his path. In January 1932, Maurice Fulton wrote longtime Kansas resident Riley Lake to learn of his fate. Lake wrote back, on Fulton's typed letter, that Middleton married Birdie Colcord, sister of the famous lawman Charles Colcord. He described Middleton as "dark complected a full face Black eys [sic] Height about 5 feet 10 inches weigh about 180 # Heavy Black Mustache, the Ear [sic] marks of a general west/tner. Very quiet.... Never was in any trouble here."[16]

While Middleton was no saint, as proved by his attempts at monetary gain through Tunstall's father, his post-Lincoln activity was primarily non-violent. This shaded the Belle Starr connection an unlikely one. His stomping grounds were in the cattle regions of Kansas, New Mexico Territory and Texas. Therefore, the greater possibility was that he returned to the cattle trade. The rumor was handy for a second Middleton, as any association with the famous Billy the Kid struck fear into men's hearts.

Another of the fortunate survivors was Sam Smith. His name caused speculation, as the sheer number of Sam Smiths in the region confused many researchers. The Regulator lived near Seven Rivers, but later purchased numerous lots in the town of Eddy. In time, this town changed its name to Carlsbad. Smith was more businessman than herdsman, and he lived a quieter life with a large family. Eve Ball wrote Phil Rasch that although "...Sam Smith was much older than she, he married Bill Jones' daughter. I tried to interview him, too late, for he was ill, bedfast, and very old. I regret that I know little about him."[17] Smith's home geographically fit with members of the Seven Rivers Gang. Despite being the last of the group to die, in 1949, he never published a memoir on his early activities. His great-grandson, Ace Clark, recalled that he kept a locked trunk in his bedroom that contained items from his youthful experiences. On top was the revolver he carried, and a fifth of whiskey.[18]

Sam B. Smith as a young man. Courtesy of Ace Clark, great-grandson of subject.

A few Regulators survived by leaving New Mexico Territory. Regulators Fred Waite and Jim French, both with connections to the Indian Territory, served as cowhands brought in by the cattle barons. Waite was from Paul's Valley, part of the Chickasaw Nation in the southern section of the Territory. Reportedly he offered the Kid a home once they both tired of Tascosa in the latter months of 1878. Although the Kid remained, Waite rebuilt his reputation and started anew.[19] In 1928, a woman named Susie Peters visited his widow and wrote Maurice Fulton of her experience.

A few days ago, I visited Mrs. Fred Waite. I had trouble in finding her, as she has hidden herself away and is little known. I wrote her several letters that she did not answer, so, I went to see her. She lives on a farm near Sulphur Springs, Okla. she is married again, and her name is Thetford; their farm is rocky and off of the main roads; her house is old-four rooms, rather bare, yet there are a few heavy pieces of old time furniture, that shows she has seen better days. They raise turkeys for the market; she has no children; she was Fred Waite's second wife, he had a daughter by his first wife, she is still living.

Fred Waite died in 1885 [1895], after a short illness; he was at that time a member of the Chickasaw Legislature, you know he was of Chickasaw blood. He was a permit collector, and practiced law in Ardmore, Okla.[20]

Ms. Peters continued her correspondence with Fulton several decades later. She doubted Waite's credential as a lawyer, but not a political appointment as collector of permits. In this position, he collected taxes on cattle, certainly something familiar to his former occupation. By 1954, Peters corrected Waite's date of death to October 24, 1895.[21]

Jim French slipped into legend. Like Middleton, he was rumored to be a lover to Belle Starr. It was difficult to prove a definite connection. "Big Jim," according to Coe, moved back to the Indian Territory. He was reportedly shot in Keota, Oklahoma in 1924. Another version of French's fate, traced by historian Mike Tower, wrote that his death actually took place in 1891. According to Mullin, reliable information placed French in South America after the Lincoln County War. Yet another version stated that French served as a soldier, and died during a fight with the famous chieftain Victorio. In all cases, French was known as a bad-tempered drunk. He was wounded during the April 1, 1878 ambush on Sheriff Brady, according to Mrs. Taylor Ealy, formerly of Lincoln. French was arrested after the murder of her friend Huston Chapman. Further, he reportedly assaulted Susan McSween in December 1878. In Mullin's notes, she claimed that Big Jim killed himself.[22]

Only a few Regulators and witnesses lived into the 1920s and 1930s. Scurlock returned to the safety of his family in Texas, dying there in 1929. He steadfastly refused to discuss the Lincoln County War. His Great-Grandsons recalled him as strict, but adamant about education— no doubt because of his own scholastic work. He moved several times in Texas. His occupation changed several times, even making money by writing college papers and contributing to textbooks. In the early 1930s, researchers sought elderly residents for their input. George Coe, who felt the Kid was misunderstood, was an essential account. Sallie Chisum, a witness and bystander, wrote years of diary entries until her death on September 12, 1934 at her home in Artesia. Alexander McSween died at the height of the Lincoln County War, but his wife Susan remarried and lived in White Oaks, a short distance from Lincoln. There she died on January 3, 1931.[23]

Some of the participants and witnesses moved elsewhere. Frank Angel completed his investigation in the late summer of 1878. His wrath concentrated on Governor Axtell, whose propaganda machine heightened tensions through his pro-"Santa Fe Ring" newspapers. Axtell used these publications to attack Angel's reputation, but these cost him. After Angel briefed President Hayes in Washington, the Governor was replaced by former soldier Lew Wallace. Ash Upson retained his position as postmaster at Roswell until February 24, 1879, although his commission was effective until October 31, 1881. He teamed with Pat Garrett in the real estate business and they remained good friends despite Upson's unquenchable penchant for drink. He resided with the aging former sheriff in Uvalde, Texas. It was there that the scribe passed away in 1894.[24]

In the final analysis, the responsibility for the three deaths in Blackwater Canyon fell to all of the Regulators—not just the Kid. Most were destined to die young given the conditions. However, Angel's conclusions proved correct: circumstantial evidence littered the investigation into Tunstall's death and the ensuing actions without assessing exactly who pulled the trigger. There were too many maybes. The ensuing actions indicated Blackwater Canyon was the real tipping point of the violence.

7

A SHOVELFUL OF FATE

Billy the Kid was never charged for the deaths of Morton or Baker. However, the death of Buckshot Roberts brought him plenty of grief. The ambush of Sheriff Brady and Deputy Hindman, on April 1, 1878, spelled plenty of trouble for the Regulators. These murders overshadowed the importance of Blackwater Draw. The full extent of this was realized by historians. Fulton wrote Mullin after Brady and Hindman died, the grand jury on the case indicted no one "on those who had participated in the killing of Morton & Baker."[1] Dick Brewer's version of events received tacit acceptance. Of course, their conclusion was ridiculous, but the grand jury opted for peace. New depredations arose, and the deaths of the three men in Blackwater Canyon became one in a line of events. In time, they became part of the legend of Billy the Kid.[2]

In 1946, Bill Hazelwood told a young rancher what he knew about the graves of the three men. He related with a wave of his arms and stated, "Those cowboys are under the rocks." One generation told the next about one of the biggest mysteries of the Lincoln County War, and yet only those two families between 1878 and the present owned the land.[3]

William Hudson Hazelwood was born on January 7, 1870 in Spring Creek, Texas, and seven years of age when his family moved to Lincoln County. They settled on the edge of Blackwater Canyon, and the young man chanced upon the Kid during one of his journeys through. He gave a silver dollar to the boy for a night's lodging in his stables. Only a short distance away, authorities sought his arrest. As the Kid was a local hero to the community, he was never refused food or lodging.[4] In fact, his friend

Francisco Trujillo revealed that the Kid and others returned to Blackwater Draw after the death of Juan Armijo nearly two months later. Trujillo related, "We then pursued our course toward the Captian [sic] mountains and arrived at Agua Negra at day break and there we had our lunch. At this point the party broke up, the Anglos going to Lincoln, the Mexicans to San Patricio..."[5]

William Hazelwood (right), longtime resident of the Blackwater Canyon area. Courtesy of Ted Clements, grandson of subject.

The loyalty of the residents in Blackwater Canyon and vicinity was beyond question. Trujillo, like many of his trusted allies, lived near several villages populated by Spanish-speaking majorities allied to the Kid. The most notable examples, San Patricio and Picacho, differed in stature. The town of Picacho lacked the notoriety given to San Patricio as a hideout for the Regulators, but was physically a more secure location. Located at the confluence of the Ruidoso and Hondo Rivers, Picacho boasted a close-knit community on the main road from Lincoln to Roswell. One of the best descriptions of the town came from Georgia Redfield, employed by the Works Progress Administration in the 1930s to conduct regional interviews on local history and folklore.

> Then came Picacho! The place I had heard least about and the spot I loved best of all. It nestled cozily in the green Hondo River Valley surrounded by the foothills that had grown higher and higher as we drew closer to the White Mountains. We lost no time in climbing Picacho Peak which gave the place its name, and is Spanish, meaning peak or summit. When we had reached the top we had a splendid view of the little town of adobe houses gayly festooned with garlands of bright red chili, and with smoke curling from the mud chimneys. We could plainly see someone walking on the long gallery of our own adobe house—the hotel and store—a mile away.[6]

Further out towards Roswell, Jim Miller described the area, and he noted there was "a large bivouc [sic] of Mexican families—some of them quite well to do sheep men—at the head of North Spring River, who were digging a large irrigation ditch with the intention of taking up and irrigating all the valley.... The Herrald [sic] War was still fresh in their minds."[7]

Redfield's description, and Miller's statement, gave a definitive reason why the Kid felt safe to kill his enemies in the Blackwater Canyon area. Redfield described Picacho accurately in its composite, but missed the political issues that Miller noted. The Horrell War, and the unsettling events in the area in 1873–74, made this area unfriendly to some while sympathetic to independent cowhands. The authorities in Lincoln already generated suspicion, and the cowhands worked and socialized with these residents. Morton and Baker, both with their homes far to the south, would not be familiar faces to the area residents.

It was no secret that the Kid courted several ladies from the Spanish families. Antonia Otero, resident of the Lincoln area whose family knew the Kid, felt area residents worked as an informal intelligence network, warning him if his enemies closed in. She provided a description of her own family memory.

> Seven brothers and four sisters lived there, one very fond of Billy the Kid. Billy the Kid really liked her, so he would get out of Lincoln and hide over there at her house … about ten miles. My grandma would feed him and then pack a lunch for him.... [She] told him to go so he would not get caught.[8]

Otero's great-aunt was one of Billy the Kid's many sweethearts, but there were several relationships such as this in the area. It was not always a friendly environment. Hondo Valley resident Joseph Gutierrez mentioned that two brothers from the Chavez family were killed in a field between San Patricio and Picacho, known as Hondo. The supposed cause was horse theft from the Regulators after trailing the Kid to Roswell. Although the Kid was blamed, the settlers in the area doubted his responsibility in the murders. It was reminiscent of the Horrells and their followers.[9]

The Hazelwood family had nothing to do with the Horrell War, but he worked for the primary businesses that settled in the area after the Lincoln County War: the 3C, Diamond, and Block Ranches. After raising four grandchildren after his daughter's early death, he worked in the saddle at an advanced age to support them. From his acreage near Blue Water Springs adjacent to Blackwater Canyon, he made homemade wine from a nearby grape patch and continued his work on the land. After his death on October 17, 1958, his land was out of family hands for a decade.[10]

Morton's family settled in different locations. Buck's brother Quin Morton became wealthy in West Virginia's coal mining industry. Not unlike his brother, he worked his way up, starting as a bookkeeper for the Turkey Knob Coal Company before organizing his own organization in 1903. He managed and organized other coal interests until his death near Charleston, West Virginia, on March 11, 1925. His daughter wrote on the family, and mentioned Buck was "killed by outlaws" without any mention of the Lincoln County War or Billy the Kid.[11]

When the family separated, Buck's sister Joanna was adopted by her relatives, Leonard and Elizabeth Anderson, in Washington D.C. She met and married Benjamin Hurxthal, a cousin to Quin's wife. Buck's generation of the Morton family ended with her death in 1949. The two letters she wrote to Fulton passed to Mullin in November 1953, but there was no record they were ever returned.[12]

Like the Mortons, tragedy struck the Beckwith family over the ensuing decades. Buck's sweetheart, Helen Beckwith, lost her brother Robert in the July fighting in Lincoln. Her father Hugh, disapproving of another daughter's marriage to a former Union soldier, murdered his own son-in-law. Her parents separated, with her mother moving with the children to Pecos County, and later to El Paso, Texas. They received good education—Helen attended school in New York, then married Captain Ferdinand Martin. After a time, she practiced nursing, as several of her sisters, in Memphis, Tennessee and Chicago, Illinois. She lived with relatives until her death on October 20, 1929. Far from most of her family, she was buried beside her sister Josephine in Florence, Alabama.[13]

The Marshall family publically broke their silence about the murders in the 1970s. Griffin's daughter Mary wrote an article for the *Hudson Review*, and a portion appeared in a 1972 issue of *True West* magazine. Both contained some factual errors, but provided valuable information. The *Hudson Review* article followed the path of the Marshall Brothers into Montana and Idaho, where they settled. She correctly concluded that Morton, although she inaccurately called him "David Morton," was killed by the Kid and the Regulators. In compiling her family history, Mary

Marshall revealed her father's flight. The fate of the two brothers differed. John was a successful businessman in Montana until his untimely death by a robber. Griffin moved to Cassia County, Idaho and married. He died on May 12, 1924, never having moved back to Virginia.[14]

Frank Angel's report was the definitive document on the Tunstall murder. U.S. Attorney General Charles Devens forwarded the report to Secretary of Interior Carl Schurz in January 1879. He asked Schurz if he agreed with Angel's findings and whether any further action was necessary. The investigation stopped, as most of the suspects and witnesses were either dead or captured. Angel suspected several in Tunstall's murder, but his conclusion proved indecisive. Depositions filled in much detail, but tainted by bias. Barring anything definitive, Attorney General Devens and Schurz passed on going any further in looking into the Tunstall murder.[15]

Tunstall's father kept his son's murder investigation alive for a time. Former Regulator John Middleton, relocated in Kansas, wrote him. Although claimed by Buck Morton to be a friend in his final letter, Middleton proved otherwise in his letters to the elder Tunstall. His goal appeared to be money. By June 1879, Middleton failed in his attempts to blame others for the younger Tunstall's murder, and he named Widenmann, Dolan, and John Chisum as the culprits. John Partridge Tunstall slowly responded to Middleton's many pleas for money. The former Regulator spoon-fed information to the old man about his son's financial interests in New Mexico Territory, but made a big mistake. In January 1880, Middleton sent a letter that invoked both the ghost of Billy the Kid and a living Jessie Evans.[16]

> Billy Bonney was with us when your son was killed. Billy held out true to our side until the last 6 months, and if reports are true, money has won him over. If it is true, I shall never have any more confidence in him. I have lost confidence in many of the boys in the way they have acted recently.... I told you about Evans assisting me, which proved to be a short loan and having to pay him his money back, leaves me almost without a dollar, and a little fifteen-year-old wife to take care of.[17]

Middleton's letters amounted to little beyond a shakedown. The last letter to the elder Tunstall, sent from Evansville, Kansas in February 1881, mentioned that New Mexico Territory was still a dangerous place. It became clear to the elder Tunstall that Middleton served him little purpose.[18]

As to the deaths of Morton, Baker, and McCloskey, they became part of the larger legend of Billy the Kid. The murders at the draw were discussed in texts on the Lincoln County War, but no conclusion cleared Morton and Baker of their own crimes completely. Their own families knew little or nothing of them. Morton's family made several unsuccessful searches in New Mexico. McCloskey's family never knew his involvement with the Regulators. If the testimony following the death of MacNab was truthful, then Baker's family tried to avenge him. However, until our expedition found the cartridges in the canyon, they were covered up, moved, and forgotten.

Much was learned of the deaths at Blackwater Draw through the personalities of the victims. Buck Morton's fate was the classic case of bad luck. He was of good family, and his writing highlighted his proper schooling. He hardly appeared the evil man mentioned in Widenmann's deposition. Completely opposite, Baker deserved his bad reputation. Trouble followed him everywhere, and illegal activity attracted him like a magnet. Of the three victims, McCloskey was the saddest case. His death was both unexpected and based on a wrong premise. Whereas Morton and Baker figured what their fate was, McCloskey had no such luxury. His advanced age, at least compared to his companions, made him a moderate voice snuffed out for little gain.

Lastly, a portion of the legend emerged from reports on the numbers of bullets in the bodies of Morton and Baker. Rasch found in the May 4, 1878 *Santa Fe New Mexican* that both men were shot eleven times. After our expedition found the bullet cartridges in 2006, we were convinced that the shots expended over time rather than all at once. Without finding an actual skeleton to inspect the physical impact, it was be difficult to discern the length of time. However, there was a profusion of bullet cartridges pooled near the encampment—the point of flight and attempted escape. This question, and the romanticism of the Lincoln County War, exists to this day.[19]

EPILOGUE:

Looking For Them

In the hot sun of July 2006, a group of us made our way through Blackwater Canyon to find clues to the murder of Buck Morton and his companions. Although the murders took place 128 years prior, rumors abounded as to the location of the bodies. It was my second time on the property. The rancher who owned the land was kind enough to allow a search of the canyon. I met retired lawman and historian Steve Sederwall and former Lincoln County Sheriff Tom Sullivan in Capitan. With them was Lonnie Lippmann, who knew much of the subject matter. Also in the group were several members of the Billy the Kid Outlaw Gang: Robert "Doc" Sproull, Ronald Hadley, and Roger Allen, who wielded the mapping system to assist our search. We met the rancher and his son at the canyon early on a sunny July morning and got to work.

The search for the three victims proved a difficult task. It took place in stages. We reviewed all available research. As I discovered, the history of the Western United States relied heavily on oral tradition, far different than my previous work in other geographic areas. The separation of "wheat from chafe" was vital to a successful study—and there was a lot of chafe. In fact, much of the basic historical account relied on published sources, which created more legend than fact. Additionally, there was general suspicion.

In 1961, the Kid's own relatives dared to shake the legend. Lois Telfer, a New York beautician and distant cousin of the outlaw, visited Lincoln and thought it proper to have her famous relative reburied there. Some disagreed, viewing Fort Sumner as the Kid's resting place. Ms.

Telfer's case died amid much acrimony. Oddly, that never stopped random visitors from chipping away at the monument for souvenirs. In fact, the oft-photographed stone that exists today was erected in the 1940s. Although a fence and gate provided minimal protection, scavengers stole the stone for a few days in 1976. The cemetery grew over with weeds. However, despite all the problems, they kept the grave in Fort Sumner. Lois Telfer must have wondered what hit her.

In the latter half of 2003, Sederwall and Sullivan experienced similar trouble. They, along with DeBaca County Sheriff Gary Graves, re-opened the Billy the Kid case using modern police applications, including the possibility of DNA comparison. While they expected some adversity, it turned into something like a second Lincoln County War. In Silver City, New Mexico, in a December 2003 hearing to exhume the body of Catherine Antrim, the Kid's mother, Sederwall presented his case in court. Instead of watching the case play out, some audience members attended in hardened opposition. It got little better over the next year and a half, as Graves was recalled. Sederwall and Sullivan decided to withdraw from any inclination to dig at Silver City or Fort Sumner. It deprived all of the possibility of finding new answers, and proved old divisions still existed.

As our small party met the rancher and his family, he loaded us into an old truck and took us down a bumpy stretch of road. Several more vehicles followed. We passed a spring and stopped near a pair of square rocks to our left. The rancher pointed to the rocks.

"That's where they are."

He related his discussions with Bill Hazelwood about the murder site. Hazelwood was nearly 88 years old when they rode together through the canyon. He passed a trusted secret between the two families—an awareness of historical caretaking. Spanish sheepherders buried the bodies, and their religious observances to the Catholic Church led me to believe that the symbolic nature of the rocks were headstones to the gravediggers.

Emerging from the cars, the search party avoided snakes and the plentiful cactus needles. The first studies around the rocks revealed a small nail from a coffin or horse. Then Ron found a lone Winchester cartridge on the surface—perhaps yards from the rocks. Later analysis revealed the round was likely not age appropriate. Little more was found at this location. Using a tripod, Lonnie snapped photographs of each find. As the day wore on, several in the party fanned out towards the spring. After a time, Doc and Sederwall shouted out. Three hundred yards from the rocks was a treasure trove. In a small space was a large cache of different bullet cartridges, metal pieces and porcelain shards. Many period cartridges were found, and we made several conclusions. First, this was an encampment and the place Billy the Kid's party stopped. Camps were used over and over, so it was necessary for a lab to look at the cartridges. Several cartridges were also found between the two locations. Sederwall has good police instincts, and he knew what this meant. "They didn't try to get away on horses. The shells meant they all took a shot at the camp and they ran towards the rocks."

The pattern of the shells proved the rocks were along the fatal path. One of the victims—Baker or Morton, neared the rock, and then fell from a rifle shot at close range. It was an eerie end, often told with the same vague details. In the rush of panic, Morton and Baker made a last chance dash from the camp, perhaps at the shock of seeing another of their captors, William McCloskey, shot dead. They knew they were next. The two ran on a vague path across the darkening canyon floor. The profusion of shells indicated that nearly all the capturing party fired a round. The lack of many cartridges at the rock meant that the victims ran there. The other already lay dead or wounded. Like the Charles M. Russell artwork showing the deaths of the two, the fugitives were not on horses but on foot.

Lonnie examined the cartridges: it appeared to him that there were a number of 44-caliber pistol cartridges, some 45-caliber Colt pistol cartridges, two 45-60 Winchester round cartridges, and two 44-40 rifle cartridges with double extraction marks. All but a few cartridges found were age appropriate, but the chemical make-up of the undisturbed ground enabled surface or upper crust finds. A large cluster of cartridges lay near a flat area just a short distance from the draw. Most of the captors were bunched in one area. Was Bill Hazelwood right? Were they buried next to the rocks?

Without digging too hastily around the rancher's property, our group gathered our finds and waited until autumn and the absence of snakes. We needed ground-penetrating radar. In October, we returned with most of the group augmented by a science team from Texas A&M University, and searched again near the rocks. The brush and vegetation grew tall from months of rain, perhaps the most the Blackwater Canyon area received in years. It proved problematic for radar equipment, but a large "x-shaped" search was conducted around the stones. The scientists crossed on each side of the rocks for fifty feet and then in a straight line around the formation. The results yielded no bones, just calcium carbonate. Old texts reveal the bodies may have been moved. The real culprit was probably the assumption that they were literally buried next to the rocks. The rancher said that Bill Hazelwood pointed out the rocks as a landmark with the sweep of his arms. They were "over there." Today they are still over there.

Pages 128 and 129. Composite of pictures from Blackwater Draw searches, July and October 2006. Courtesy of Julie Baker Carter.

REPORT OF ANALYSIS, AGRA NEGRA SPRINGS

Adapted from Report of Analysis, Case No. 2003-274 Lincoln County, New Mexico

Offense: Triple Homicide

Offense Location: Agua Negra Springs, Lincoln County, NM

Victim:Frank Baker, William "Buck" Morton, William McCloskey

Examiner: Michael G. Haag

Date: 6/26/2008

Introduction:

At the request of Deputy Sheriff Steve Sederwall, Lincoln County Sheriff's Office, a number of corroded and damaged, fired cartridge casings were examined in order to determine possible caliber types, as well as to evaluate the potential existence of microscopic marks from a firearm.

Results:

Many of the items submitted are in damaged and corroded condition, altering original manufactured measurements to various degrees. Several casings possess headstamp information, but most do not. Those with headstamp information can be more specifically identified as a particular caliber. At the request of Steve Sederwall, none of the cartridge casings were cleaned or altered.

Caliber determinations were primarily based on measurements of rim diameter, diameter of the case near the rim, and overall case length.

All intact items examined were centerfire casings, with normal appearing firing pin impressions.

Bag #1

The corroded, damaged casing from this bag possesses a headstamp indicating it is a Union Metallic Cartridge (UMC) brand, 45-60 Winchester caliber cartridge casing. The headstamp present on this straight walled cartridge casing indicates it was manufactured prior to 1900.

[Note: The casing was thought to be introduced in 1879, associated with the Winchester model 1876 lever action rifle. However, there is a remote possibility a version may have been in use the previous year.]

Bag #2

Bag #2 contains a total of four fired, corroded and damaged cartridge casings. None of these items possess headstamps, but are consistent with 45 Colt (also referred to as 45 Long Colt) caliber cartridge casings. This caliber of cartridge casing was introduced in 1873. Many firearms have been chambered for this caliber, particularly the Colt, Single Action Army revolver for the time period in question. These cartridge casings show few original or remaining marks from firearms that might be used for comparison purposes.

Bag #3

This bag contained three fired, damaged and corroded cartridge casings and two metal fragments. The two fragments are from unknown calibers/cartridges. The largest cartridge casing has no headstamp, but is the same caliber as the lone cartridge casing from bag #1, a 45-60 Winchester. This particular cartridge casing shows few original or remaining marks on the head and primer which might be used for comparison purposes; however, there are two possible extractor override marks on the rim which might be of value for comparison. The last cartridge casing from this bag possesses no headstamp, and has been crushed to a significant extent. For this reason, the exact caliber cannot be determined; however, the most likely caliber candidates are 38 Special and 38 Long Colt... The 38 Long Colt cartridge was introduced in 1875.

Bag #4

Bag #4 contained a total of two fired, damaged and corroded cartridge casings without headstamps. While one is in better condition that [sic] the other, they both appear to be the same caliber. Based on the dimensions of these items, they are the most consistent with either 45 Auto Rim (45 Automatic Rim) or 44 Smith & Wesson Russian caliber casings.

The Auto Rim cartridge was introduced in 1920. The 44 Smith & Wesson Russian cartridge was introduced in 1870. Because the 45 Auto Rim cartridge was produced in a period when headstamps were more common, the likelihood of these items being 44 Smith & Wesson Russian may be higher.

Several indentations on the rims of these casings (indicated above) could possibly be used for comparison purposes with cleaning. These markings could be from rimfire firing pins (caliber mismatch), extractor over ride, or some other unknown interaction. Additionally, possible marks of value for comparison are present in the primer metal backflow.

Bag #5

A total of twenty five fired cartridge casings in various condition were found in bag #5. Two of these possessed headstamps. One indicated the brand as Winchester Repeating Arms Company, caliber 45 Colt (caliber described above for Bag #2). The second headstamp indicated Winchester Repeating Arms brand, but 44 Winchester Center Fire caliber, which is also known as 44-40 Winchester, or 44 Winchester. The 44-40 Winchester cartridge was introduced in 1873, and was originally closely associated with the Winchester model 1873 lever action rifle. In this group of twenty five casings, eighteen are most consistent with 44-40 Winchester caliber, and seven are most consistent with 45 Colt caliber. Some of these cartridge casings possess potential marks for comparison purposes.

Results:

Caliber determination was primarily based on measurements of rim diameter, diameter of the case near the rim, and overall case length.

Bag #6

Bag #6 was found to contain a single, fired, damaged and corroded cartridge casing possessing no headstamp. This item is most consistent with 45-70 Government (45 Government) caliber. This caliber was introduced in 1873. Through the late 1800's, this cartridge was most often associated with the Springfield Model 1873 rifle (Trapdoor Springfield). This cartridge casing does possess some potential comparative marks of value in the primer metal back flow. Additionally, should cleaning of this item be allowed at a later time, evaluation of the firing pin impression might yield a more comprehensive understanding of the type of firearm that may have been used to discharge this cartridge. If a Trapdoor type rifle was used, an angled firing pin impression would be expected. Given the current condition of this cartridge casing, this Examiner has no opinion on the type of firearm used.

[Note: This was the bullet found at the Tunstall scene approximately 2-3 inches below the surface. It was examined at the same time as the cartridges collected from Blackwater Canyon.]

The conclusions drawn by examiner Michael Haag are scientific in nature and do not match the cartridges to a particular person's weapon. Yet these were period weapons and the location they were found make it almost certain. The above-mentioned request was started in 2006, but the final report was released in 2008. Also note that there was a different version of weapon used to fire several of these which would date the cartridges earlier than appearances would have it.

BIBLIOGRAPHICAL SUMMARY ON SOURCES

This work contained as much fresh primary source material as could be located. As previously explained, this is not always possible, as some "piggy-backing" is unavoidable in studies of the Lincoln County War. Source material was sought outside of the immediate area. As a result, among the new sources utilized was material from Mr. Ted Clements, Vado, New Mexico; a previously unknown letter from Frank MacNab, courtesy of Ms. Carol Rogers, Lake City, Kansas; discussions with and material examined from Ms. Sallie Chisum Robert, Great-Granddaughter of Sallie Chisum Robert; the Bouldin Family Papers, Virginia Historical Society; Notes and materials from the Morton Family, including Charles Morton, his brother David Holmes Morton, and their cousin, the late Sallie Wilson and her daughter Helen Payne; the Margaret Marshall Papers, Beinecke Library, Yale University; and material from Harold Beckwith, Florence, Alabama. In learning about the possible lineage of William McCloskey, I contacted Jean Ter Har of Oregon and her brother Jim Squires of Texas. Further material on the Hondo Valley emerged from interviews with Joseph Gutierrez, Hondo, New Mexico, and with Mr. and Mrs. Herman Otero, Capitan, New Mexico.

To prevent reliance on previous hypothesis, I consulted several primary source collections vital to the original documents. These included the exceptional Robert N. Mullin Collection in the Haley Memorial Library and History Center, Midland, Texas; the Weisner and Myers Papers, Rio Grande Historical Collections at the New Mexico State University, Las Cruces, New Mexico; the Lily Klasner Papers in the L. Tom Perry Special Collections, Harold B. Lee Library, Brigham Young University, Provo, Utah;

the Phil Rasch Papers, Lincoln Heritage Trust, Lincoln, New Mexico and the Hubbard Museum of the American West, Ruidoso Downs, New Mexico; the Fulton Papers at the University of Arizona Special Collections; the Works Progress Administration Interviews held at the Manuscript Division of the Library of Congress, and the Angel Report originals at the National Archives, College Park, Maryland. Other primary source collections that contributed to the work included the John Nathan Hittson Papers, Texas Tech University's Southwest Collection; and the Donald Cline Papers, New Mexico State Archives.

Newspaper sources were plentiful, but those in New Mexico Territory were largely utilized for political gain or airing grievances. Other newspapers revealed genealogical information pertinent to the account. Those used in the research for this work included the *Mesilla Independent; Mesilla News; Santa Fe New Mexican; Baird (Texas) Star; Albuquerque Review; Roswell Daily Record; El Paso Times; Daily Enquirer & Examiner (Virginia); Sedalia (Missouri) Daily Democrat; Denver Daily Times; Reserve Advocate; Barber (Kansas) Index; Dodge City Times;* and the *Charleston (West Virginia) Daily Mail.*

The two key published accounts that garnered the most reference material related to the work of Maurice Fulton. His 1927 edition of Pat F. Garrett's *The Authentic Life of Billy the Kid* is considered the most important version of this work. The first edition, published in 1882, lacked Fulton's insight. For many years, it was accepted as the "official" version of events, although it was well known Ash Upson was the ghostwriter on a number of chapters. It was largely his account that dominated the deaths of Morton, Baker, and McCloskey. Facts and documentation dominated Robert N. Mullin's *Maurice Garland Fulton's History of the Lincoln County War.* Painstaking details are abundant in Mullin's work, based on findings and correspondence with Maurice Fulton until the latter's death in 1955. The reason for the reliance on Fulton and Mullin is a fact-based relation that avoids unnecessary "piggy-backing" of more modern-day theory. It's a "back to basics" approach that draws directly from the first minds that documented it.

Despite emphasis on Fulton and Mullin, a number of superior accounts abound. These include Doyce R. Nunis' edition of George Washington Coe's *Frontier Fighter*; Miguel Antonio Otero's *The Real Billy the Kid*; William Lee Hamlin's *The True Story of Billy the Kid*; Helen Wilson's unpublished compilation, entitled *Life and Genealogy of Quin Morton*, Virginia Historical Society; Charlotte County Board of Supervisors, *Charlotte County—Rich Indeed: A History from Prehistoric Times Through the Civil War*; Eve Ball's edition of Lily Klasner's *My Girlhood Among Outlaws*; Robert K. DeArment's edition of Phil Rasch's news articles, *Warriors of Lincoln County*; Frederick Nolan, *The Life and Death of John Henry Tunstall*; Bob Boze Bell, *The Illustrated Life and Times of Billy the Kid*; Al Erwin's *The Southwest of John H. Slaughter*; and Robert M. Utley, *Billy the Kid-A Short and Violent Life*. Other books integral to this account, but including more specific references, included Mike Tower's *The Outlaw Statesman—the Life and Times of Fred Tecumseh Waite*; Billy Charles Patrick Cummings' *Frontier Parish—Recovered Catholic History of Lincoln County, 1860–1884*; Ed Bartholomew's *Jesse Evans, A Texas Hide-Burner*; Maurice G. Fulton, *Roswell in its Early Years*; Emerson Hough, *The Story of the Outlaw—A Study of the Western Desperado*; Frederick Nolan, *Bad Blood—The Life and Times of the Horrell Brothers*; Frazier Hunt, *The Tragic Days of Billy the Kid*; W.W. Mills, *Forty Years at El Paso 1858–1898*; Beatrice Grady Gay, *Into the Setting Sun—A History of Coleman County* [Texas] ; C.L. Sonnichsen, *El Paso Salt War*; James Shinkle's edition of *Reminiscences of Roswell Pioneers*; and Walter Noble Burns, *The Saga of Billy the Kid*.

Magazine articles and journal sources that provided support included Max Coleman's "Never Fool with a Fool," *Frontier Times* (January 1936); Margaret Marshall, "What was your name in the States?" *True West* (June 1972); Margaret Marshall, "An American Memoir," *Hudson Review* (Summer 1971); Philip J. Rasch, "The Horrell War," *New Mexico Historical Review* (July 1956); Robert N. Mullin, "Here Lies John Kinney," *Journal of Arizona History* (1973); Harwood P. Hinton, Jr., "John Simpson Chisum, 1877–84," *New Mexico Historical Review* (July 1956); Various 1979 and 1980 issues of *Tinnie's Silver Dollar Historical Roundup*; and Lee Scott Thiesen, ed.,

"Frank Warner Angel's Notes on New Mexico Territory, 1878," *Arizona and the West* (Winter 1976). Of these, the Marshall accounts were vital to revealing the early movement of Buck Morton and his cousins.

There will be, in time, more revealed about the biographies of the three victims and their assailants through both primary and secondary sources. As this is not a finished story, but a work in progress, future research will adjust or add to the findings presented. Of course, the greatest source of all would be the bodies of Morton, Baker, and McCloskey. Hopefully there will be finality.

NOTES

PROLOGUE

How the Blackwater Murders Started the Lincoln County War

1. Robert N. Mullin, ed., *Maurice G. Fulton's History of the Lincoln County War* (Tucson, Arizona: University of Arizona Press, 1968), 13.
2. For more on the Santa Fe Ring, see [George W. Coe] Doyce B. Nunis, Jr., ed., *Frontier Fighter—The autobiography of GEORGE W. COE who fought and rode with Billy the Kid* (Chicago, IL: R.R. Donnelley & Sons Company, 1984), xxxii-xxxviii; Biographical notes on Catron, Dolan, Elkins, Fritz, Murphy, and Riley in Coe, *Frontier Fighter*.
3. Biographical notes on John Simpson Chisum, in Coe, *Frontier Fighter*, 320.
4. Ibid., Biographical notes on John Henry Tunstall, 347.
5. Ibid., Biographical Notes on Richard M. Brewer, 315.
6. Ibid., Biographical Notes on Alexander A. McSween and Susan Ellen McSween, 334–337. Mrs. McSween's maiden name, "Hummer," was mistakenly published as "Hunter."

CHAPTER 1: THE CANYON MEANS DEATH

1. Typescript of Letter, W.S. Morton to H.H. Marshall, March 8, 1878, in Mullin, ed., *Fulton's History*, 139-140; Ibid., 141.
2. Ibid., 141; Notes, Robert N. Mullin Collection, J. Evetts Haley Library, Midland, Texas; Francisco Gutierrez, p. 284A, line 32, Precinct No. 2, Lincoln County, New Mexico Territory Census of Population, Census of the United States, 1870 (National Archives Microfilm Publication M593, roll 894) Records of the Bureau of the Census, Record Group 29.
3. This was directly taken from Maurice G. Fulton, *Roswell in its Early Years* (Roswell, New Mexico: Hall-Poorbaugh Press, Inc., 1963), 28. See Fulton's edition of Pat Garrett, *Authentic Life of Billy the Kid-The Noted Desperado* (New York, NY: The Macmillan Company, 1927), 65-66.

4. Typed Letter from *Mesilla Independent*, March 16, 1878, with notations, from Maurice G. Fulton Papers, Collection Number MS-057, Folder 7, University of Arizona Special Collections, Tucson, Arizona. Hereafter this is noted as "Fulton Papers."

5. Ibid.

6. Francisco Trujillo Interview, "Billy the Kid," May 10, 1937, in Edith Crawford, comp., Works Progress Administration (WPA), Life Histories, Folder A719, Translated by A.L. White, Manuscripts Division, Library of Congress, Washington, D.C.

7. Deposition of John Middleton, in Frank Warner Angel, *In the Matter of the Investigation of the Charges Against S.B. Axtell Governor of New Mexico*, Case No. 44-4-8-3, Records of the Department of Justice, Record Group (RG) 60, National Archives and Records Administration, College Park, Maryland. Hereafter referenced as "Angel Report."

8. Coe, *Frontier Fighter*, 132.

9. Trujillo, "Billy the Kid," May 10, 1937, WPA Files, Manuscripts Division, Library of Congress. Also see Deposition of Middleton, Angel Report, RG 60, National Archives.

10. Mullin, ed., *Fulton's History*, 175-176.

11. Mike Tower, "Big Jim French and the Lincoln County War," *Wild West*, December 2004, 34–35; Mike Tower, *The Outlaw Statesman—The Life and Times of Fred Tecumseh Waite* (Bloomington, Indiana: Authorhouse, 2007), 40. This was drawn from the Florencio Chaves Interview, Mullin Collection, Haley Memorial Library, Midland, Texas.

12. Mullin, ed., *Fulton's History*, 141–142.

13. Fulton, *Roswell in its Early Years*, 27.

14. Fulton, *Roswell in its Early Years*, 28; Garrett, *Authentic Life*, xiv–xv.

15. Miguel Antonio Otero, *The Real Billy the Kid* (New York: R.R. Wilson, Inc., 1936), 49. A new edition was published by Sunstone Press, Santa Fe, New Mexico, in 2007.

16. Otero, *Real Billy the Kid*, 49-50. You can tell there are disparities in even "official" versions of the deaths. Morton and Baker were on foot, and after the murders, it was not clear if the assailants showed up in Lincoln right away or not. Only Brewer was likely to be present.

17. Charles Marion Russell (1864-1916) was the first artist to depict the murders in printed form. The original is at the Arizona West Galleries, Scottsdale, Arizona.

18. Testimony from William Bonney on Richard Brewer's Return of Warrants in William Lee Hamlin, *The True Story of Billy the Kid-A Tale of the Lincoln County War* (Caldwell, Idaho: Caxton Printers, Ltd., 1959), 47-48.

19. Ibid.; Otero, *Real Billy the Kid*, 50; Author's Field Notes, Morton Search, Author's Collection.

20. *Albuquerque Review*, March 30, 1878, Vol. II, No. 48, 2, in Donald Cline Collection of New Mexico history research materials, collection 1959-032, New Mexico State Archives, Santa Fe, New Mexico. This is hereafter noted as "Donald Cline Collection." See Middleton Deposition, Angel Report, RG 60, National Archives.

21. Ibid.

22. Max Coleman, "Never Fool With a Fool," *Frontier Times*, Vol. 13, No. 4, January 1936, 218–219.

23. Billy Charles Patrick Cummings, *Frontier Parish—Recovered Catholic History of Lincoln County, 1860-1884* (Lincoln, New Mexico: Lincoln County Historical Society, 1995), 44-45; Field Notes, Morton Search, October 13, 2006, Author's Collections.

24. *Albuquerque Review*, March 30, 1878, in Donald Cline Collection, New Mexico State Archives.

25. J.M. Miller, "Memories of Fifty Years Ago In the Pecos Valley by One Who Has Lived Here Since 1878," *Roswell Daily Record*, March 5, 1928, Roswell Public Library. Morton's friend Milo Pierce was the person who gave Miller the account of the burial. There are several sources for this article.

26. Notes From John Meadows' manuscript, "Early Experiences," Mullin Collection, Haley Library; Files on William S. Morton & Frank Baker, Mullin Collection, Haley Library.

27. Notes on Miller, "Memories of Fifty Years Ago," *Roswell Daily Record*, March 5, 1928, in Mullin Collection, Morton & Baker Files, Haley Library, Midland, Texas.

28. Fulton, *Roswell in its Early Years*, 30.

29. Ibid.; Miller, "Memories of Fifty Years Ago," *Roswell Daily Record*, March 5, 1928.

30. The author discussed this with Ms. Sallie Chisum Robert, the great-granddaughter of Sallie Chisum. Her father was the descendant who donated the diaries to the museum in Artesia, New Mexico.

CHAPTER 2: A VIRGINIA BOY GOES WEST

1. Buck's middle name is believed to be Scott. William S. Morton, pg. 208, line 32, Charlotte Court House, Charlotte County, Virginia Census of Population, Census of the United States, 1860 (National Archives Microfilm Publication M653, roll 1340) Bureau of the Census, RG 29; Helen F. Wilson, comp., *The Life and Genealogy of Quin Morton*, typescript, ca. 1930, unpublished, in the Caperton Family Papers, Mss1 C1716a 769, Virginia Historical Society (hereafter referred to as "VHS"); Alexander Brown, D.C.L., *The Cabells And*

Their Kin (Franklin, NC: Genealogy Publishing Service, Randolph W. Cabell, 1994), 586; "George Nash Morton," in Lyon Gardiner Tyler, LL.D., ed., *Encyclopedia of Virginia Biography, Vol. V* (New York: Lewis Historical Publishing Company, 1915), 1006; D.H. Morton to T.T. Bouldin, January 21, 1868, Bouldin Family Papers, Mss1 B6638, VHS. One noted Cabell home is available to tour. Point of Honor, in Lynchburg, Virginia, was owned by Morton's Great-Grandfather.

2. Timothy S. Ailsworth, Ann P. Keller, Lura B. Nichols and Barbara R. Walker, comp., *Charlotte County-Rich Indeed: A History from Prehistoric Times through the Civil War* (Charlotte County, Virginia: Charlotte County Board of Supervisors, 1979), 304–307.

3. Ailsworth, Keller, Nichols, and Walker, comp., *Charlotte County*, 416–417; Ibid., 288; Account Books and Licenses, David Holmes Morton Papers, Mss1 M8466a,VHS; David H. Morton, pg. 208, line 30, Charlotte C.H., Charlotte County, Virginia Census of Population,1860, M653, roll 1340, National Archives.

4. Wilson, *Life and Genealogy*, VHS; Buck, named "William S. Morton," was listed in a printed summons from the Sheriff of Orange County, Virginia, dated February 15, 1878, in Commonwealth of Virginia v H.H. Marshall, et al., VHS.

5. W.S. Morton to H.H. Marshall, March 8, 1878, as published in Mullin, ed., *Fulton's History*, 139–140;Wilson, *Life and Genealogy*, Caperton Family Papers, VHS.

6. Ailsworth, Keller, Nichols, and Walkers, comp., *Charlotte County*, 477; Ibid., 228; Wilson, *Life and Genealogy*, Caperton Family Papers, VHS; D.H. Morton to T.T. Bouldin, January 21, 1868, Bouldin Papers, VHS; E-Mail, Charles Morton to Author, March 15, 2004.

7. Wilson, *Life and Genealogy*, Caperton Family Papers, VHS; *Daily Enquirer and Examiner*, May 5, 1869, Virginia State Archives, Richmond, Virginia; Gene Hile McKinney, "Shooting in Charlotte Court House," *Southsider*, Volume XIII, No. 2, 1994, 26-30; Margaret Marshall, "What was your Name in the States?," *True West*, June 1972, 7-9; Margaret Marshall, "An American Memoir," *Hudson Review*, Volume XXIV, No. 2, Summer 1971, 227. The writing on the original letters noted the actual date was 1869, not 1867. Charlotte Court House news accounts confirm it was 1869. Also, Buck was mistakenly called David Morton.

8. *Daily Enquirer and Examiner*, May 5, 1869, Virginia State Archives; Marshall, "What Was Your Name," *True West*, June 1972, 9; McKinney, "Shooting in Charlotte Court House," *Southsider*, 26–33.

9. Wilson, *Life and Genealogy*, VHS; Marshall, "What Was Your Name," *True West*, June 1972, 8–9; G.S. Marshall to Mary Gaines, May 29, 1869, letter in Marshall, "An American Memoir," *Hudson Review*, 227–228; Morton Notes, in

Mullin Collection, Haley Library; Joanna Hurxthal to Maurice Fulton, June 1, 1928, in Morton Notes, Mullin Collection, Haley Library; James Wilmer Stith, pg. 569B, line 27, Subdivision No. 1, Carondelet, St. Louis County, Missouri Census of Population, Census of the United States, 1870 (National Archives Microfilm Publication M593, roll 809) Bureau of the Census, RG 29.

10. Griffin Stith Marshall to Mary Gaines, in "An American Memoir," *Hudson Review*, 228. The date is actually May 29, 1869, not May 29, 1867. The original letter is in the Margaret Marshall Papers, Yale Collection of American Literature, Beinecke Rare Book and Manuscript Library, New Haven, Connecticut. Hereafter this referred to as "Beinecke Library."

11. Ibid.; James Stith, pg. 569B, Carondelet, St. Louis County, Missouri Census of Population, 1870, M593,roll 809, RG29, National Archives; Entry of Simon Taylor, St. Louis, Missouri Death Records, Volume IV, 118. See June to Margaret Marshall, June 3, 1948, Margaret Marshall Papers, Yale Collection of American Literature, Beinecke Library.

12. William Morton and Samuel P. Daniel, pg. 70, lines 1 & 13, Wylliesburg, Charlotte County, Virginia Census of Population, Census of the United States, 1870 (National Archives Microfilm Publication M593, roll 1640) Bureau of the Census, RG 29; D.H. Morton to T.T. Bouldin, January 21, 1868, Bouldin Family Papers, VHS.

13. Morton to Bouldin, January 21, 1868, Bouldin Family Papers, VHS.

14. Morton and Daniel, 1870 Charlotte County, Virginia Census of Population, M593, roll 1640, RG 29, National Archives; Samuel Daniel, pg. 27, line 27, Cross Timbers, Hickory County, Missouri Census of Population, Census of the United States, 1860 (National Archives Microfilm Publication M653, roll 623), Bureau of the Census, RG 29.

15. Wilson, *Life and Genealogy*, Caperton Family Papers,VHS; Marshall, "What Was Your Name," *True West*, June 1972, 9; M.F. Cabell to Thomas T. Bouldin, January 15, 1871, Bouldin Family Papers, VHS.

16. James Stith, pg. 569B, Carondelet, St. Louis County, Missouri, Census of Population, M593, roll 809, RG 29, National Archives; Fannie Taylor [Stith], pg. 314B, line 6, Turner's District, Fauquier County, Virginia Census of Population, Census of the United States, 1850 (National Archives Microfilm Publication M432, roll 943) Bureau of the Census, RG 29; St. Louis City Death Records, Vol. 4, Pg. 118; Robert Barnes, "Thorowgood Stith: Mayor of Baltimore, 1804–1808," *The Archivists-Bulldog*, Vol. 13, No. 9, 3; *Sedalia Daily Democrat*, Vol. 1, No. 271, November 13, 1872; *Sedalia Daily Democrat*, Vol. 9, No. 22, January 15, 1873.

17. D.H. Morton to Maurice Fulton, December 6, 1927, Fulton Papers, University of Arizona Special Collections.

18. Joanna Morton Hurxthal to Maurice G. Fulton, June 1, 1928, in notes, Mullin Collection, Haley Library.

19. J.M. Miller, "Memories of Fifty Years Ago," *Roswell Daily Record*, March 5, 1928, in Notes, Mullin Collection, Haley Library; James M. Miller, "Sheep Ranching on the Chisum Cattle Range," in Shinkle, ed., *Reminiscences of Roswell Pioneers* (Roswell, New Mexico: Hall-Poorbaugh Press, Inc., 1966), 25–26; "James M. Miller," Manuscript, Rio Grande Historical Collections, New Mexico State University, Las Cruces, New Mexico.

20. Hurxthal to Fulton, June 1, 1928, in notes, Mullin Collection, Haley Library.

21. Corbett, Hoye & Co.'s Second Annual Denver City Directory for 1874, 249; Corbett, Hoye & Co.'s First Annual City Directory for 1873, 243; *Denver Daily Times*, February 26, 1873, Denver Public Library; *Denver Daily Times*, December 15, 1873, Denver Public Library.

22. *Denver Daily Times*, November 26, 1873, Denver Public Library; Ed Bartholomew, *Jesse Evans, A Texas Hide-burner* (Houston, Texas: Frontier Press of Texas, 1955), 19; Robert N. Mullin to Phil Rasch, April 28, 1956, Rasch Papers, Lincoln Heritage Trust, Lincoln, New Mexico. Copies found in Hubbard Museum of the American West, Ruidoso, New Mexico.

23. Open Letter by Robert A. Widenmann, March 30, 1878, *Cimarron News and Press*, in Mullin, ed., *Fulton's History*, 154.

24. Lewlie to Maille [Mary William Bouldin], February 20, 1875, Bouldin Family Papers, VHS.

25. Ibid.

26. Coe, *Frontier Fighter*, 57–58; Eve Ball, ed., Lily Klasner, *My Girlhood Among Outlaws* (Tucson, Arizona: University of Arizona Press, 1972), 169–170.

27. "The Kid," Manuscript in Lily Casey Klasner Papers, L. Tom Perry Special Collections, Harold B. Lee Library, Brigham Young University. Portions of this appear in Klasner, *My Girlhood*, 170.

28. Entry of John Simpson Chisum, in Coe, *Frontier Fighter*, 320; Klasner, *My Girlhood*, 170.

29. Susan E. Barber to Maurice Fulton, March 10, 1928, Fulton Papers, University of Arizona Special Collections.

30. Klasner, *My Girlhood*, 67–68.

31. Ibid.; W.S. Morton to H.H. Marshall, March 8, 1878, as quoted in Mullin, ed., *Fulton's History*, 140; Ibid., 137; Mike Tower, "Big Jim French and the Lincoln County War," *Wild West*, December 2004, 34.

32. Klasner, *My Girlhood*, 59–60.

33. Bob Mullin to Phil Rasch, April 11, 1954, Herman B. Weisner Papers, Rio Grande Historical Collections, Archives & Special Collections Department, New Mexico State University, Las Cruces, New Mexico.

34. Mullin, ed., *Fulton's History*, 140.

35. Marshall, "An American Memoir," *Hudson Review*, 225–226; The sibling Charles Marshall was found in Charlotte County Records within days of his brother's death. See Charlotte County, Virginia, Deed Book 35, 342. This

was more likely Griffin Marshall, given his accuracy in relating Morton's death; Marshall, "An American Memoir," *Hudson Review*, 230–231.

36. Notes on Seven Rivers, New Mexico, Mullin Collection, Haley Library; "A Story of the Early Days in the Cattle Business in Texas and NEW MEXICO," *The Reserve Advocate*, October 4, 1922.

37. Phil Rasch with Lee Myers, "The Tragedy of the Beckwiths," from *English Westerners' Brand Book*, Vol. 5, No. 4, July 1963, in Robert K. DeArment, ed., *Warriors of Lincoln County* (Laramie, Wyoming: National Association for Outlaw and Lawmen History, Inc., 1998), 78; Ibid., 75.

38. Notes, from letter attributed to Laura Beckwith Oliver, Undated, Lee Myers Papers, Rio Grande Historical Collections, New Mexico State University Special Collections.

39. Klasner, "The Kid," in Klasner Papers, L. Tom Perry Special Collections, Harold B. Lee Library, Brigham Young University.

40. Rasch with Myers, "Tragedy," in DeArment, *Warriors of Lincoln County*, 75–76. The Beckwith Ranch was located near the present-day village of Lakewood, New Mexico.

41. "Cattle Thievery and Morton Estate," *Mesilla News*, June 8, 1878, in Donald Cline Collection, New Mexico State Archives.

42. Copy, Inventory of Property of Estate of William Morton, Deceased, from Weisner Papers, Rio Grande Historical Collections, New Mexico State University. Original located in Lincoln County Courthouse, Carrizozo, New Mexico.

43. Administrative Statement, September 6, 1880, from Weisner Papers, Rio Grande Historical Collections, New Mexico State University.

44. Myers Notes, from letter attributed to Laura Beckwith Oliver, Undated, from Myers Papers, Rio Grande Historical Collections, New Mexico State University.

CHAPTER 3: TWO HIDDEN LIVES

1. Fulton, *Roswell in its Early Years*, 29.
2. Ibid.
3. Marshall A. Upson to Florence Downs, March 15, 1878, Fulton Papers, University of Arizona Library Special Collections.
4. Phillip J. Rasch, "The Horrell War," *New Mexico Historical Review*, Vol. 31, No. 2, July 1956, 223; Ibid., 226–227; Ibid., 230.
5. Ibid., 223–226. Emerson Hough, *The Story of the Outlaw—A Study of the Western Desperado* (New York: The Outing Publishing Company, 1907), 201; For a full detailed study on the Horrell War, see Frederick Nolan, *Bad Blood-The Life and Times of the Horrell Brothers* (Stillwater, Oklahoma: Barbed Wire Press, 1994).

6. Klasner, *My Girlhood*, 105-106; Ibid. 175.
7. "Little" Hart Notes, Mullin Collection, Haley Library; Klasner, *My Girlhood*, 181-182.
8. Robert Mullin to Phil Rasch, December 10, 1955, Rasch Papers, Lincoln Heritage Trust.
9. Robert N. Mullin, "Here Lies John Kinney," *Journal of Arizona History*, Vol. 14, No. 3 (1973), 226.
10. Entry of "Simeon Hart" in W.W. Mills, *Forty Years at El Paso 1858-1898* (El Paso, Texas: Carl Hertzog, 1962), 182; Audubon R. Davis, Bucks County Historical Society to Maurice G. Fulton, December 16, 1952, Mullin Collection, Haley Library; Upson to Downs, March 15, 1878, Fulton Papers, University of Arizona Special Collections.
11. Frazier Hunt, *The Tragic Days of Billy the Kid* (New York, NY: Hastings House, 1956), 42. A New Edition was published by Sunstone Press, Santa Fe, 2009.
12. Aaron H. Hart, Pg. 336, line 27, Palo Pinto, Palo Pinto County Census of Population, United States Census of Population, 1860 (National Archives Microfilm Publication M653, roll 1302) Bureau of the Census, RG 29; Palo Pinto County, Texas, Probate Minutes, Estate Case File 168, Palo Pinto County Courthouse; "Progressiveness and Bravery Revealed in History of County," *Baird Star*, December 10, 1937, Southwest Collection, Texas Tech University Special Collections, Lubbock, Texas; Hart Family, Pg. 333B, line 12, Enumeration 176, Precinct No. 2, Callahan County, Texas Census of Population, United States Census of Population, 1880 (National Archives Microfilm Publication T9, roll 1294) Bureau of the Census, RG 29; Joseph Carroll McConnell, *The West Texas Frontier or a Descriptive History of Early Times in Western Texas* (Palo Pinto, Texas: Texas Legal Bank & Book Co., 1939), 105; Ibid., 78; Report No. 21, B.F. Baker Estate Exhibit, Palo Pinto County, Probate Book A, 187, Palo Pinto Courthouse, Texas.
13. "W.W. Hunter Gives Sketches of his Life," in Beatrice Grady Gay, *"Into the Setting Sun"—A History of Coleman County* (Santa Ana, Texas: 1939), 85–86.
14. Affidavit of James Hart, Indian Depredation Claims, in John Nathan Hittson Papers, hereafter called "Hittson Papers," Southwest Collection, Texas Tech University Special Collections; Report to Commissioner of Indian Affairs, Hon. D.C. Atkins, Indian Depredation Claims, in Hittson Papers, Southwest Collection, Texas Tech University Special Collections; Brands of Hart and A.H. Hart, Brand Book, Palo Pinto County, Texas.
15. Trujillo, "Billy the Kid," May 10, 1937, Works Progress Administration Papers, Manuscripts Division, Library of Congress.
16. Baker Family, Pg. 364A, line 9, Enumeration District 45, Cuero, DeWitt County, Texas Census of Population, United States Census of Population, 1880 (National Archives Microfilm Publication T9, Roll 1299) Bureau of the Census, RG 29.

17. Mullin, "Here Lies John Kinney," *Journal of Arizona History*, 226.
18. A.M. Gildea to Maurice G. Fulton, July 15, 1930, Fulton Papers, University of Arizona.
19. Klasner, *My Girlhood*, 175–176.
20. Mullin, ed., *Fulton's History*, 67; Mullin, "Here Lies John Kinney," *Journal of Arizona History*, 227; Philip J. Rasch, "The Reign of the Boys," *Real West*, June 1980, in DeArment, ed., *Warriors of Lincoln County*, 199; William D. Reynolds, "Frank Baker: Forgotten Gunman of the Lincoln County War," from Donald Cline Collection, New Mexico State Archives; No. 13 S. Schutz to Second Assistant Secretary of State, July 13, 1877, in "El Paso Troubles in Texas— Letter from the Secretary of War," in *House of Representatives, Executive Document No. 93, 45th Congress, 2d Session* (Washington, D.C.), 136–137.
21. Otero, *The Real Billy the Kid*, 42.
22. Ibid.
23. Reynolds, "Frank Baker," Donald Cline Collection, New Mexico State Archives.
24. Ibid.
25. Ibid.; Mullin, ed., *Fulton's History*, 84–86.
26. "Grand Reunion of "The Boys," *Mesilla Independent*, in Mullin, ed., *Fulton's History*, 86-87.
27. Ibid.
28. Ibid.
29. Mullin, ed., *Fulton's History*, 84–85; Ibid., 87; Reynolds, "Frank Baker," from Donald Cline Collection, New Mexico State Archives.
30. Letter of D.H. Ewing, *Mesilla Independent*, October 20, 1877, in Mullin, ed., *Fulton's History*, 88.
31. Ibid.
32. Mullin to Rasch, March 27, 1955, Rasch Papers, Lincoln Heritage Trust; Letter of "Order," *Mesilla Independent*, October 20, 1877, in Mullin, ed., *Fulton's History*, 88–89; Entry of "George Warden Peppin," in Coe, *Frontier Fighter*, 340-341.
33. Frederick Nolan, *The Life and Death of John Henry Tunstall* (Albuquerque, New Mexico: University of New Mexico Press, 1965), 250–251. A New Edition with Corrections and Additions was Published by Sunstone Press, Santa Fe, 2009; Mullin to Rasch, March 27, 1955, Rasch Papers, Lincoln Heritage Trust.
34. Nolan, *Tunstall*, 252–253. Another difference between the accounts of Nolan and Mullin was the date of escape. Mullin placed it at November 16, while Nolan has it around November 7.
35. Letter to Editor from "Lincoln," *Mesilla Independent*, in Mullin, ed., *Fulton's History*, 89-90. Despite the obvious quip at security, "Lincoln" was referring to the Seven Rivers Gang. Andy Boyle, called "Pasha," was a deputy sheriff in the county.

36. Mullin, "Here Lies John Kinney," *Journal of Arizona History*, 227-228; C.L. Sonnichsen, *El Paso Salt War* (Carl Hertzog and the Texas Western Press at the Pass of the North, 1961), 58–59; *Mesilla Independent*, December 29, 1877, Rio Grande Historical Collections, New Mexico State University Special Collections; Barber to Fulton, March 10, 1928, Fulton Papers, University of Arizona Special Collections.

37. Coe, *Frontier Fighter*, 132.

38. Obituary, Mrs. John Durfee, *Barber Index*, May 26, 1938; Carol Rogers to Author, January 7, 2007, Author's Collections.

39. Letter Attachment, Carol Rogers to Author, January 7, 2007, Author's Collections; Entry of April 29, 1878 in Bob Boze Bell, *The Illustrated Life and Times of Billy the Kid* (Phoenix, Arizona: Tri-Star-Boze Publications, Inc., 1996), 68. The letter was sent from "Ms. Sallie Chisum" to "Miss Lizzie M. Lester, Syracuse, Kansas." Fifteen was designated as the letter number between the correspondents. Ron Cooke, another descendant, related the account of the family's settlement.

40. Copy of Letter, Frank Macnab to Lizzie Lester, April 19, 1878, in Carol Rogers to Author, January 7, 2007, Author's Collections. This letter has never been published before.

41. "Frank Macnab Heard From," *Dodge City Times*, July 7, 1877.

42. Bartholomew, *Jesse Evans*, 13.

43. Notes, Klasner Papers, Tom Perry Special Collections, Harold B. Lee Library, Brigham Young University.

44. William McCloskey, Pg. 730B, line 26, Precinct No. 1, Valencia County, New Mexico Territory Census of Population, United States Census of Population, 1870 (National Archives Microfilm Publication M593, roll 897) Bureau of the Census, RG 29; Bartholomew, *Jesse Evans*, 13; William McCloskey, Pg. 864, line 183, Troy, Doniphan County, Kansas Territory Census of Population, United States Census of Population, 1860 (National Archives Microfilm Publication M653, roll 347) Bureau of the Census, RG 29; Sarah McCloskey, Pg. 4A, line 74, LaPlata, San Juan County, New Mexico Territory Census, United States Census of Population, 1910 (National Archives Microfilm Publication T624, roll 917) Bureau of the Census, RG 29; Edward C. McCloskey, Pg. 4B, line 49, LaPlata, San Juan County, New Mexico Territory Census, 1910, T624, roll 917, Bureau of the Census, RG 29.

45. "Notes Made from Indian Bureau Files, Washington Relating to Mescalero Agency Affairs 1873–1878," in Eve Ball Papers, Tom Perry Special Collections, Harold B. Lee Library, Brigham Young University.

46. McCloskey Notes, Mullin Collection, Haley Library; *Mesilla News*, February 12, 1876, Rio Grande Historical Collections, New Mexico State University; Phil Rasch, "George Washington of Lincoln County," in DeArment, ed., *Warriors of Lincoln County*, 38-39.

47. McCloskey Notes, Mullin Collection, Haley Library; Walter Noble Burns, *The Saga of Billy the Kid* (New York, NY: Grosset & Dunlap, 1926), 89.

CHAPTER 4: THE TUNSTALL MURDER WHODUNIT

1. Sherry Robinson and Eve Ball, *Apache Voices: their stories of survival as told to Eve Ball* (Albuquerque, New Mexico: University of New Mexico Press, c.2000), 125; Ibid., 129–130.
2. Ibid., 127.
3. Copy of Cheque, Weisner Papers, Rio Grande Historical Collections, New Mexico State University; Mullin, ed., *Fulton's History*, 63; Ibid., 104–107.
4. "A Tax-Payer's Complaint," Office of John H. Tunstall, January 18, 1878 to Editor of the *Independent*, in Angel Report, RG 60, National Archives.
5. "Answer to Tax-payer's Complaint," Newspaper Clipping, Angel Report, RG 60, National Archives.
6. Statement of James J. Dolan, Angel Report, RG 60, National Archives; Mullin, ed., *Fulton's History*, 107–108.
7. Ibid., 108.
8. Deposition of Robert Widenmann, Angel Report, RG 60, National Archives.
9. Deposition of J.B. Mathews, Angel Report, RG 60, National Archives; Deposition of John Hurley, Angel Report, RG 60, National Archives.
10. Deposition of Widenmann, Angel Report, RG 60, National Archives.
11. Ibid.
12. Ibid.
13. Deposition of Mathews, Angel Report, RG 60, National Archives.
14. Deposition of Charles Kreiling, Angel Report, RG 60, National Archives; Deposition of Mathews, Angel Report, RG 60, National Archives.
15. Deposition of Mathews, Angel Report, RG 60, National Archives.
16. Deposition of Kreiling, Angel Report, RG 60, National Archives.
17. Ibid.
18. Ibid.
19. Ibid. Kreiling misspelled Hindman as "Hardeman."
20. Ibid.
21. Deposition of Mathews, Angel Report, RG 60, National Archives.
22. Ibid.
23. Depositon of Kreiling, Angel Report, RG 60, National Archives; Deposition of Widenmann, Angel Report, RG 60, National Archives; Buck Morton Notes, Mullin Collection, Haley Library.
24. Deposition of Widenmann, Angel Report, RG 60, National Archives.
25. Deposition of Hurley, Angel Report, RG 60, National Archives.

26. Deposition of Robert W. Beckwith, Angel Report, RG 60, National Archives.
27. Summary of Frank W. Angel, Angel Report, RG 60, National Archives; Memorandum for the Chief Clerk and Administrative Assistant, R.M. Moore, Acting Chief, Department of Justice, Division of Mail and Files, RG 60, National Archives. The latter appeared to be done for the convenience of Maurice Fulton, who was looking into the Angel Report.
28. "The Inquest on J.H. Tunstall," in Grady E. McCright and James H. Powell, "Disorder in Lincoln County: Frank Warner Angel's Reports," *Rio Grande History*, No. 12, 1981, New Mexico State University, unnumbered.
29. Ibid.; Mullin, ed., *Fulton's History*, 137–138.
30. Robert Mullin to Phil Rasch, December 5, 1954, Rasch Papers, Lincoln Heritage Trust; "Recovery of Spent Cartridge at Tunstall Murder Site," April 22, 2005, Lincoln County Sheriff's Department Supplemental Report, Case 2003–274.

CHAPTER 5: CAPTURE AND TRAIL TO BLACKWATER

1. Otero, *The Real Billy the Kid*, 46.
2. *Santa Fe New Mexican*, May 4, 1878, in Mullin Collection, Haley Library.
3. Notes, Mullin to Phil Rasch, June 12, 1957, Mullin Collection, Haley Library; Al Erwin to Mullin, Undated, Mullin Collection, Haley Library; Mullin, ed., *Fulton's History*, 138.
4. Miller, "Memories of Fifty Years Ago," *Roswell Daily Record*, March 5, 1928; "The Inquest on J.H. Tunstall," unnumbered, in McCright and Powell, "Disorder in Lincoln County," *Rio Grande History*, New Mexico State University; Morton Notes, Mullin Collection, Haley Library.
5. Erwin to Rasch, June 12, 1957, Mullin Collection, Haley Library.
6. Ibid.; Al Erwin, *The Southwest of John H. Slaughter* (Glendale, California: A.H. Clark Co., 1965), 125. Erwin included the capture of Morton and Baker in his description of the Howell family. Cap Howell, a Missourian and former Confederate soldier, needed a fresh start after the Civil War. He panned gold in Montana and farmed in Nevada before herding livestock. At the Pecos River, he kept his cows on the New Mexico side. They lived in a dugout constructed by a sheepherder. Morton, Baker, and Cochran hid out at the Howell Place, as they knew the family well. Judging from the description given by Erwin, Cochran was most familiar with the Slaughters.
7. Hunt, *Tragic Days of Billy the Kid*, 42.
8. Ibid.; Miller, "Memories of Fifty Years," *Roswell Daily Record*, March 5, 1928.
9. Hunt, *Tragic Days of Billy the Kid*, 42-43.
10. Pink Simms to Maurice Fulton, May 16, 1932 in "Personal Characteristics" File, Mullin Collection, Haley Library.

11. Ibid.

12. Garrett, *Authentic Life*, 62.

13. Ibid., 62–63.

14. Burns, *Saga of Billy the Kid*, 86–87.

15. List of "Presents," Copy of Sallie Chisum Diary, 1878, 142, Courtesy of Sallie Chisum Robert. The original is at the Artesia Museum, Artesia, New Mexico. The two cameo hearts were given August 13, 1878; the ring given at Fort Sumner around August 28th; Pictures of "Emelio" and Peter Maxwell on August 23rd.

16. Harwood P. Hinton, Jr., "John Simpson Chisum, 1877–84," *New Mexico Historical Review*, Vol. XXXI, No. 3, July 1956, 189–190.

17. Burns, *Saga of Billy the Kid*, 88; Coe, *Frontier Fighter*, 132. It might be noted that Sallie Chisum Robert, great-granddaughter of Sallie, told the author that the diary was donated to the museum library in Artesia, New Mexico, by her father William Robert. Copies, or at least partial copies, were in the Rio Grande Historical Collections, New Mexico State Library in Las Cruces.

18. Coe, *Frontier Fighter*, 132.

19. Ibid.

20. Hand Drawn Map by Will J. Chisum in Letter, January 17, 1940, Subject Files, Mullin Collection, Haley Library.

21. Upson Family Association of America, comp., *The Upson Family in America* (New Haven, CT: The Tuttle, Morehouse & Taylor Company, 1940), 179; Marshall Ashley Upson, "The Hondo Valley, And Roswell In The 1870's and 1880's," in Shinkle, ed., *Reminiscences of Roswell Pioneers*, 8–9.

22. Ash Upson, "The Hondo Valley," in Shinkle, ed., *Reminiscences*, 9–10; Ibid, 11–15.

23. Ibid., 15.

24. Florence E.D. Muzzy to Maurice Fulton, March 16, 1928, Fulton Papers, University of Arizona Special Collections.

25. Hough, *Story of the Outlaw*, 210.

26. Garrett, *Authentic Life*, 63–64.

27. Ibid., 64; "From Lincoln County THREE MEN Killed," Typed Copy, Mesilla *Independent*, March 16, 1878, Fulton Papers, University of Arizona Special Collections; Burns, *Saga of Billy the Kid*, 89.

28. Otero, *Real Billy the Kid*, 48.

29. Miller, "Memories of Fifty Years Ago," *Roswell Daily Record*, March 5, 1878.

30. Ibid.

31. J.M. Miller to Allen Sears, Undated, Mullin Collection, Haley Library.

32. Her remaining papers are in the possession of her Great-Granddaughter, Sallie Chisum Robert.

33. Morton Notes, Mullin Collection, Haley Library; W.S. Morton to H.H.

Marshall, March 8, 1878, in Mullin, ed., *Fulton's History*, 139–140.

34. Morton to Marshall, March 8, 1878, as quoted in Mullin, ed., *Fulton's History*, 139-140.

35. Garrett, *Authentic Life*, 63.

36. Henry V. Gaines to Margaret Marshall, January 7, 1964, Margaret Marshall Papers, Yale Collection of American Literature, Beinieke Library.

37. Miller, "Memories of Fifty Years Ago," *Roswell Daily Record*, March 5, 1878.

38. Clipping of Newspaper, *Mesilla Independent*, with letter, April 21, 1878, in Angel Report, National Archives. The writer was thought to be Widenmann, who was in the vicinity.

39. "Arabela—A Place of Tranquility," *Tinnie's Silver Dollar Historical Roundup*, Winter 1980, Vol. 11, No. 1 (Roswell, New Mexico), 2; "Lincoln County's Oldest Citizen Lived at Arabella," *Tinnie's Silver Dollar Historical Roundup*, Summer 1979, Vol. I, No. 3, 1; Ibid., 6; "He was a Likeable Person" Billy the Kid Not Forgotten!," *Tinnie's Silver Dollar Historical Roundup*, Summer 1980, Vol. II, No. 3, 8. The compiler of this material, historian Clarence S. Adams, spent his childhood in the area and interviewed many local residents. Tinnie's Silver Dollar is a working restaurant in the Hondo Valley.

CHAPTER 6: DAMNATION OF THE REGULATORS

1. Lee Scott Thiesen, ed., "Frank Warner Angel's Notes on New Mexico Territory, 1878," *Arizona and the West*, 18 (Winter 1976), 333–334; Ibid., 350.

2. Robert M. Utley, *Billy the Kid—A Short and Violent Life* (Lincoln, Nebraska: University of Nebraska Press, 1989), 64–65; Ibid., 67; Ibid., 72; A.N. Blazer, "Fight at the Blazer Mill," *Alamogordo News*, August 16, 1928, 14–16. Original in Rio Grande Collections, New Mexico State University; Utley, *Billy the Kid*, 78–79; Ibid., 157–159.

3. Jessie Evans Notes, Rasch Papers, Lincoln Heritage Trust; Bartholomew, *Jesse Evans*, 70–72.

4. Undated Clipping in Exhibit 17, Angel Report, RG60, National Archives.

5. Bob Mullin to Phil Rasch, October 25, 1953, Copy in Weisner Papers, Rio Grande Historical Collections, New Mexico State University; Mullin, ed., *Fulton's History*, 213–214.

6. "The Lincoln County War," *Mesilla Independent*, ca. May 2, 1878, Copy in Weisner Papers, Rio Grande Historical Collections, New Mexico State University.

7. Frank McNab File, Mullin Collection, Haley Library.

8. Original Notes from Francisco Trujillo's account to WPA, May 10, 1937, in Frank McNab File, Mullin Collection, Haley Library.

9. Ibid.; Mullin, ed., *Fulton's History,* 213; *Cimarron News and Press,* May 4, 1878, in Mullin, ed., *Fulton's History,* 217.

10. *Santa Fe New Mexican,* May 10, 1878, in Mullin, ed., *Fulton's History,* 220.

11. Notes from Interview, Harold and Mike Stewart, Eastland, Texas, January 10, 2009, Author's Collections; Mullin, ed., *Fulton's History,* 225–226; "Proclamation By the Governor," in Mullin, ed., *Fulton's History,* 229; Entry of Peppin, in Coe, *Frontier Fighter,* 340-341; Mullin, ed., *Fulton's History,* 267.

12. Phil Rasch to Bob Mullin, October 24, 1953, in Weisner Papers, Rio Grande Historical Collections, New Mexico State University.

13. Colin W. Rickards, "More on Henry Newton Brown," *English Westerners Brand Book,* Vol. 3, No. 1, October 1960, 8. Clipping from Weisner Papers, Rio Grande Historical Collections, New Mexico State University; Nyle H. Miller and Joseph W. Snell, *Great Gunfighters of the Kansas Cowtowns, 1867-1886* (Lincoln, Nebraska: University of Nebraska Press, 1963), 50; Ibid., 62–63.

14. Rickards, "More on Henry Newton Brown," *English Westerners Brand Book,* 8–9; Miller & Snell, *Great Gunfighters,* 54–63.

15. Nolan, *Life and Death of Tunstall,* 275–276; Philip J. Rasch, "These Were the Regulators," in Robert DeArment, ed., *Warriors of Lincoln County,* 189–190; Edwin P. Hicks, *Belle Starr and Her Pearl* (Little Rock, AR: Pioneer Press, 1963), 60–65; Ibid., 111. The original letters between Middleton and J.P. Tunstall are in the Fulton Papers, University of Arizona Special Collections.

16. Maurice Fulton to Riley Lake, January 18, 1932, Mullin Collection, Haley Library; Lake to Fulton, Undated, Mullin Collection, Haley Library.

17. [Eve Ball] to Phil Rasch, ca. 1955, Rasch Collection, Lincoln Heritage Trust.

18. Notes, Eve Ball Papers, L. Tom Perry Special Collections, Harold B. Lee Library, Brigham Young University, Provo, Utah; Interview, Ace Clark, Reno, Nevada, November 13, 2008, Author's Collections.

19. Coe, *Frontier Fighter,* 347–348; Mike Tower, "Big Jim French and the Lincoln County War," *Wild West,* December 2004, 34. For further information, see Mike Tower, *The Outlaw Statesman,* 46–47.

20. Susie Peters to Maurice Fulton, October 1, 1929, Fulton Papers, University of Arizona Special Collections. 1885 was a mistake, as Waite died in October 1895.

21. Susie C. Peters to Maurice Fulton, December 1954, Fulton Papers, University of Arizona Special Collections.

22. Hicks, *Belle Starr,* 60; Mike Tower, "Big Jim French and the Lincoln County War," *Wild West,* December 2004, 36–37; James Hansel French Notes, Mullin Collection, Haley Library. Mrs.[Susan McSween] Barber to Fulton, Nov. 23, 1928, Mullin Collection, Haley Library.

23. Grave of Josiah G. "Doc" Scurlock, Eastland City Cemetery, Eastland County, Texas; Interview, Mike and Harold Stewart, Eastland, Texas, January 10, 2009,

Author's Collections; Marshall Bond, *Gold Hunter* (Albuquerque, New Mexico: University of New Mexico Press, 1969), 174–175; Georgia B. Redfield, "Rare Photograph of Sallie Chisum Obtained by Historian in Roswell After Long Search," *El Paso Times*, April 12, 1953, Myers Papers, Rio Grande Historical Collections, New Mexico State University; "Mrs. Barber Only 87 and Billy Did Not Kill M'Sween, Says Z.F. Zimmerman, Her Nephew," *Santa Fe New Mexican*, January 6, 1931.

24. Theisen, "Frank Warner Angel's," *Arizona and the West*, 336–337; William A. Keleher, *Violence in Lincoln County 1869-1881—A New Mexico Item* (Albuquerque, New Mexico: University of New Mexico Press, 1957), 177–178. A new edition was published by Sunstone Press, Santa Fe, New Mexico, 2007; "Demands for an Inquiry," in McCright and Powell, *Disorder in Lincoln County*, 9–10; Notes on M.A.Upson, Donald Cline Collection, Archives of New Mexico; John A. Haley, *A History of Lincoln County Post Offices-Folklore and Tales About People and Postmasters in Early Southeastern New Mexico* (Ruidoso, New Mexico: Ruidoso Printing Company, 1976); T.U. Taylor to Major Maurice G. Fulton, February 5, 1940, Rasch Papers, Lincoln Historical Trust.

CHAPTER 7: A SHOVELFUL OF FATE

1. Morton Notes, "Pertaining to Killing Morton & Baker," Mullin Collection, Haley Library.
2. Ibid.; Notes on Charges, Donald Cline Collection, New Mexico State Archives.
3. Interview, John Cooper, Arabella, New Mexico, July 21, 2009, Author's Collections.
4. Interview with Ted Clements, Vado, New Mexico; Notes, "William Hudson (Bill) Hazelwood and Meddie Alice (Purcella) Hazelwood and Their Two Children," Courtesy of Ted Clements.
5. Trujillo, "Billy the Kid," May 10, 1937, Works Progress Administration Collection, Manuscripts Division, Library of Congress.
6. Georgia B. Redfield, "Coming to Roswell In Stage Coach Days," in Shinkle, ed., *Reminiscences of Roswell*, 198.
7. Miller, "Memories of Fifty Years Ago," *Roswell Daily Record*, March 5, 1928.
8. Interview, Antonia Otero, May 16, 2007, Author's Collections. Her husband is related to Governor Miguel Otero. Her grandmother was Antonia Padilla.
9. Interview, Joseph Gutierrez, Hondo, New Mexico, July 20, 2009, Author's Collections.
10. Interview with Ted Clements, Vado, New Mexico; "William Hudson (Bill) Hazelwood," Courtesy of Ted Clements.
11. "Quin Morton, Prominent Coal Operator, is Called by Death," *Charleston*

Daily Mail, March 11, 1925; Wilson, *Morton Family,* Caperton Family Papers, Virginia Historical Society.

12. Interview, Sallie Wilson, Hilton Head, South Carolina, March 2007, Author's Collections; D. Holmes Morton to Maurice G. Fulton, December 6, 1927, Fulton Papers, University of Arizona Special Collections; Josephine [Morton] Anderson, Pg. 92, line 22, Washington City First Ward, District of Columbia Census of Population, United States Census of Population,1870 (National Archives Microfilm Publication M593, roll 123) Bureau of the Census, RG 29; Joanna Morton, Pg. 413, line 23, Enumeration District 16, New Castle County, Delaware Census of Population, United States Census of Population, 1880 (National Archives Microfilm Publication T9, roll 119) Bureau of the Census, RG 29; Cousin Fannie to D.Q. Eggleston, December 17, 1882, Eggleston Papers, Manuscripts Department, University of Virginia Library; Greenbrier County, West Virginia, Marriage Register, 1-B, 105, Greenbrier County Courthouse; Morton Notes, Mullin Collection, Haley Library; Maurice Fulton to Robert Mullin, November 6, 1953, Fulton Papers, University of Arizona Special Collections.

13. Refugia Beckwith, Pg. 497, line 33, Enumeration District 119, Pecos County, Texas Census of Population, United States Census of Population, 1880 (National Archives Microfilm Publication T9, roll 1323), Bureau of the Census, RG 29; Helen B. Martin, Pg. 6B, line 98, Memphis Ward 2, Shelby County, Tennessee Census of Population, United States Census of Population, 1920 (National Archives Microfilm Publication T625, roll 1763) Bureau of the Census, RG 29; Rasch with Myers, "Tragedy," in DeArment, ed., *Warriors of Lincoln County,* 85; Helen Beckwith Grave, City Cemetery, Florence, Alabama. The 1920 Census noted an incorrect age for Helen Martin, but correctly noted relationship to her sister Camelia Olinger.

14. Marshall, "An American Memoir," *Hudson Review,* summer 1971, XXIV, 2, 226–230; Marshall, "What was your name?" *True West,* 7–8. Ibid., 232–233; Ibid., 226; Entry of Griffin Marshall, Idaho Death Index, 1911–51, Idaho Department of Health and Welfare, Boise, Idaho.

15. "In the Matter of the Cause and Circumstances of the Death of John H. Tunstall, a British Subject," in Angel Report, RG 60, National Archives. The Angel Report was forwarded on January 10, 1879. See Attorney General Charles Devens to Secretary of the Interior Carl Schurz, January 10, 1879, Angel Report, RG 60, National Archives.

16. John Middleton to J.P. Tunstall, June 17, 1879, Fulton Papers, University of Arizona Special Collections; John Middleton to J.P. Tunstall, January 19, 1880, Fulton Papers, University of Arizona Special Collections. See Nolan, *Life and Death of Tunstall,* 259–270.

17. Middleton to Tunstall, January 19, 1880, Fulton Papers, University of Arizona Special Collections.

18. John Middleton to J.P. Tunstall, February 9, 1881, Fulton Papers, University of Arizona Special Collections.
19. Phil Rasch to R.N. Mullin, December 10, 1954, in Weisner Papers, Rio Grande Historical Collections, New Mexico State University.

Breinigsville, PA USA
08 February 2011
255087BV00001B/10/P

9 780865 347809